Advance Praise for *Solutionomics*

"*Solutionomics* breaks America's stubborn political divide in a refreshing way. It illustrates how simple, yet powerful changes in economic incentives and Congressional transparency can motivate CEOs and politicians, both Republican and Democrat, to elevate the competitiveness of the U.S. economy, raise the earning potential of American workers, and reset American democracy so that it once again drives national prosperity."

—Philip T. Powell, Faculty Chair, Kelley School of Business, Indiana University

"*Solutionomics* is a must-read guide for educating the American public about the current state of our economy and offers some intriguing solutions that can help us rebuild the American Dream."

—Cary Correia, Chief Commercial Data Science Leader, General Electric

SOLUTIONOMIC$

INNOVATIVE SOLUTIONS FOR ACHIEVING AMERICA'S ECONOMIC POTENTIAL

CHRIS MACKE

A POST HILL PRESS BOOK
ISBN: 978-1-64293-096-2
ISBN (eBook): 978-1-64293-097-9

Solutionomics:
Innovative Solutions for Achieving America's Economic Potential

Cover art by Cody Corcoran

The information and advice herein is not intended to replace the services of financial professionals, with knowledge of your personal financial situation. The advice and strategies contained herein may not be suitable for your situation. You should consult with a professional where appropriate. Neither the publisher nor author shall be liable for any loss of any profit or any other commercial damages, including, but not limited to special, incidental, consequential, or other damages. All investments are subject to risk, which should be considered prior to making any financial decisions.

Post Hill Press
New York • Nashville
posthillpress.com

Published in the United States of America

With immense gratitude to my family, friends, mentors, and teachers who collectively made this book possible.

TABLE OF CONTENTS

INDEX OF SOLUTIONS

years, and this would be retroactive to 2017, the year the Tax Cut and Jobs Act was passed. Pg. 74

Corporate Tax Solution #7: If overseas profits are used to hire more Americans, overseas profits would be taxed at a lower rate. Conversely, if the profits aren't used to hire more Americans, the tax rate would remain the same. Pg. 74

Corporate Tax Solution #8: Corporations qualifying for corporate tax cuts receive the reduced rate *after* they increase wages and/or increase their number of full-time employees. Pg. 74

Corporate Tax Solution #9: Only full-time employees that have been employed by the company for a full year count toward a company's full-time employee list, and the end-of-the-year count will be used to determine whether the full-time employee list was increased. Pg. 75

Corporate Tax Solution #10: Corporations track and report the increase/decrease in their number of U.S. full-time employees, average wage paid for U.S full-time employees, whether they converted any full-time employees to independent contractors, and whether they outsourced any full-time employees. Pg. 75

Corporate Tax Solution #11: States that are net recipients of federal dollars and offer any type of financial incentive to attract or retain companies immediately repay the difference between what they send to Washington and what they receive from Washington, with interest. Pg. 84

Corporate Tax Solution #12: Packaging for products sold in America, regardless of the company nationality, prominently displays what percentage of the total employees (including subcontractors and independent contractors) utilized in the production of the product are American-based. Pg. 84

Global Trade Solution #1: At a minimum, negotiate equal trade terms and, ideally, negotiate more favorable terms for the U.S. Pg 100

Global Trade Solution #2: Selectively and gradually leverage tariffs and quotas to first level the global playing field and then tilt to America's advantage. Pg 112

Global Trade Solution #3: This is the same as Corporate Tax Solution #11. Packaging for products sold in America, regardless of the company nationality, prominently displays the percentage of employees (including subcontractors) utilized in the production of the products that are American-based. Pg 127

Global Trade Solution #4: Create a ranking of the most patriotic companies selling goods and services in the U.S., regardless of nationality. Pg 127

Global Trade Solution #5: All costs to the American taxpayer of the government, federal, state, and local, procuring goods overseas versus in America, including lost American wages and associated taxes, health care benefits, unemployment costs, welfare, and other government assistance are factored in when governments weigh whether to buy American or from a foreign source. This will ensure the shareholders of USA Inc. get a better return on their taxpayer dollars. Pg 143

Global Trade Solution #6: When evaluating the merits of having other countries make things we are or could be making, assess whether we have an equal number of jobs that pay at least as much. Pg 147

Global Trade Solution #7: Companies selling goods and services in the U.S. publish quarterly how many American-based jobs they eliminated, how many they sent overseas or subcontracted to overseas subcontractors, the wages lost, benefits lost, and the welfare collected by the American employees who lost their jobs. Companies also track how many jobs they created in America, the wages gained, benefits gained, and reduction in welfare. Then we can get a real accounting of the impact of outsourcing versus hiring in America. Pg 152

Global Trade Solution #8: Create a patriotic company ranking system. Pg 153

Rank the patriotism of companies selling goods in the U.S., based on the percentage of each company's employees involved in producing the U.S.-sold goods in the U.S., the wages paid relative to competitors, and health care benefits provided. Pg 153

Global Trade Solution #9: Similar to Corporate Tax Solution numbers 3, 4, and 5, tie company tax rates to the rate of job creation in America. This will provide an incentive for companies to keep more jobs in America. Pg 153

Global Trade Solution #10: If foreign governments require companies selling goods in their countries to make the goods in their country, we do the same. Pg 153

Global Trade Solution #11: Eliminate Most Favored Nation status. Pg 153

Financial Crises Solution #1: Base non-salary compensation of executives and those approving loans at federally insured financial institutions and systemically important financial institutions, as designated under the Dodd-Frank Act "SIFI," on how much of the money they lend is repaid. This would ensure that our primary interest, them getting our money back and ensuring a stable source of loans, is also their primary interest. Pg 188

Financial Crises Solution #2: Pay the non-salary compensation of executives and those approving loans at federally insured financial institutions and SIFIs as they get our money back, not up front. The slower the loans get paid back, the slower they get paid. This would make our interest, getting our money back in a timely manner, the banks' interest. While banks could still make interest only and payment in kind loans, there would be less of an incentive to make them, because they wouldn't get fully paid until the loans were repaid, replacing instant gratification with ROI-based compensation. Pg 191

Financial Crises Solution #3: Penalties are in an amount equal to all the profits earned from the behavior plus 20 percent, ensuring that the profit from taking the risk is eliminated and, critically, that there is a deterrent. These funds will be placed into a system-wide bailout fund. Pg 194

Financial Crises Solution #4: Remove executives from federally insured financial institutions and SIFIs cited for infractions, and bar them from working in the financial services industry or as lobbyists for a period of ten years. Require that an amount equal to all the compensation paid to the executive during the last five years, and compensation owed in the future, be paid by the lending institution into the same bailout fund previously mentioned. Pg 194

Financial Crises Solution #5: If a federally insured financial institution or SIFI requires additional capital to continue operations, the shareholders don't provide the additional capital, no other private source of capital is obtained, and a bailout is deemed necessary to avoid a financial crisis, ownership of the lending institution goes to the taxpayers and all its shareholders are wiped out. Pg 195

Financial Crises Solution #6: If the previously mentioned bailout fund does not have enough money to bail out troubled institutions, require the other federally insured financial institutions and SIFIs to provide the necessary funding. The amount contributed by institutions to the bailout would be based on what each institution's assets represent as a percent of the total federally insured assets in our financial system. Pg 195

Financial Crises Solution #7: Permit the Federal Reserve to obtain the information it requests, so long as the information is not already being sent to another regulator. Pg 198

Financial Crises Solution #8: Require members of Congress serving on finance-related committees or subcommittees to complete a minimum number of continuing education hours on how our financial system works, along with specialized seminars relating to the various sectors of our financial system. For example, members who serve on the House Subcommittee on Housing and Insurance would attend seminars on the housing industry and insurance industry while members of the House Subcommittee on Monetary Policy and Trade would be required to earn a minimum number of continuing education hours related to monetary policy and trade. Importantly, these would not be taught by lobbyists or banks, but rather by academics. Pg 200

Expanding the Middle Class Solution #1: Support programs proven to successfully teach and enhance the technical and work-related success skills that are critical for success in the work environment. Pg 223

Expanding the Middle Class Solution #2: Annually review program results measuring improvement in hiring and retention rates; pay increases as compared to pay before entering the program; and employer satisfaction, increasing money for programs achieving the desired results and eliminating funding for programs not achieving required results. Pg 224

Expanding the Middle Class Solution #3: Increase Pell Grant funding to the most effective institutions while eliminating funding for the most costly and ineffective institutions. Pg 240

Expanding the Middle Class Solution #4: Taxpayer funding going to for-profit colleges is subject to meeting rigorous ROI evaluation concerning whether students complete the program and earn high enough wages to justify the investment and pay back their student loans. Pg 251

Expanding the Middle Class Solution #5: Ensure that potential students can view the costs and expected benefits from a program in a simple and standardized format, allowing them to make better and more informed decisions. Pg 251

Expanding the Middle Class Solution #6: Counseling by an independent third party that helps students understand the financial aid packages and student loan obligations can potentially decrease the very high loan default rate for students at for-profit colleges. Pg 252

Congressional Solution #1: Require members of Congress to receive their health care from the lowest-rated VA hospital located in their district or state and go to the back of the queue of veterans waiting for services. Pg 265

Congressional Solution #2: Require members of Congress to serve as teacher's aides one month of every year they are in office, in the lowest-achieving school in their district or state. Here is the irony: It wouldn't be surprising if they were the first teacher's aide the school had in years due to limited school funding. Pg 265

Congressional Solution #3: Members of Congress shall only vote on bills if they attended the hearings pertaining to the bill…and more than five minutes of the hearings. Pg 266

Congressional Solution #4: Members of Congress shall be required to read a detailed summary of each bill they vote on and certify that they agree with the key provisions outlined in the summary. The summaries should be provided by a non-partisan source, much like the Congressional Budget Office provides independent budget and economic analysis. Pg 267

Congressional Solution #5: Congress shall exempt itself from no law passed and imposed on We the People. Pg 268

Congressional Solution #6: Base congressional salary increases on the rate of increase in the bottom tenth's inflation-adjusted weekly earnings. Pg 269

Congressional Solution #7: Cut congressional pensions when public-sector pensions are cut, and in the same proportions. Pg 269

Congressional Solution #8: Congressional pensions are cut when, and in the same proportion, cuts are made to Social Security. Pg 270

Congressional Solution #9: If means testing for Social Security payments is implemented, members of Congress should also have their Social Security payments means tested, and the factors used to evaluate their financial means should include their congressional pensions and government-subsidized health care, among other factors. Pg 270

Congressional Solution #10: Prohibit members of Congress and staffers from working as lobbyists for the greater of five years or half the number of years they were members or congressional staffers. Pg 272

Congressional Solution #11: Members of Congress shall be held to a legal standard of a fiduciary, having a legal duty to act solely in the interest of all the people they represent, not just a few, and certainly not themselves. Pg 273

Congressional Solution #12: Require members of Congress to track the time they spend on campaign-related matters, including but not limited to fundraising, campaign events, and travel time. Pg 274

Congressional Solution #13: Develop and implement a searchable online database that allows We the People to monitor how much time members of Congress are spending on campaign-related matters. Pg 274

Congressional Solution #14: Create and implement an online comparison tool, complete with scorecards for each member of Congress, ranking them against their fellow members in time spent on campaign-related matters. Pg 274

Congressional Solution #15: Install biometric sensors that members of Congress use to enter and exit their offices, the various committee conference rooms, various member office buildings, and the House or Senate chamber. Pg 275

Congressional Solution #16: Record, store, and provide online access, in a searchable format, to every congressional member's work email. Record information about congressional staffers' work-related accounts too. They should have nothing to hide. Pg 275

Congressional Solution #17: Record, store, and provide online access, in a searchable format, to every congressional member's and staffer's phone system. Pg 276

Congressional Solution #18: Members of Congress wear NASCAR-type suits of their sponsors, otherwise known as largest campaign donors, with logos proudly displayed. Pg 276

Congressional Solution #19: Implement reverse-gerrymandering. Draw districts such that the greatest number of districts possible are evenly divided among registered voters of the Republican and Democratic parties. Pg 281

Congressional Solution #20: Implement mail-in voting in all congressional districts. Pg 282

Congressional Solution #21: Implement same-day registration in all congressional districts. Pg 282

Congressional Solution #22: Randomly assign committee chairmanships and committee assignments. Pg 286

Congressional Solution #23: Require campaign donations to be made before committee chairmanships and assignments are determined. Pg 287

Congressional Solution #24: If donors give money to members of Congress that are subsequently assigned to committees that impact the donor's industry or business, the member must return the money to the donor. Pg 288

INDEX OF GLOBAL TRADE MYTHS

INTRODUCTION

1. SOLUTIONS, NOT POLITICS

Solutionomics is about solutions, not politics. It is written for the benefit of the American taxpayer, not a political party or special interest group. It is not another book cataloging our problems with only a few of the same old platitudes and campaign talking points at the end of the book as an afterthought. Instead, *Solutionomics* contains *specific solutions* for achieving America's economic potential. The result is an action plan that will increase the financial opportunity and security of the American taxpayer, increase company revenues, and reduce our federal deficits.

The result is an action plan that will increase the financial opportunity and security of the American taxpayer, increase company revenues, and reduce our federal deficits.

Included are solutions for:

- **Winning the game of global trade**
  Solutionomics reveals the twelve global trade myths keeping America from winning the game of global trade and the truths we should be basing our trade policy on instead.

- **Creating an incentive-based corporate tax policy**
  Discover why making company tax cuts contingent on companies hiring more Americans and raising wages would generate stronger job and wage growth at a lower cost to American taxpayers.
- **Expanding the American middle class**
  Solutionomics outlines key ingredients in growing the American middle class, including increasing labor force utilization rates and getting a better return on the investment in postsecondary education for the American taxpayers funding it.
- **Reducing frequency and severity of financial crises**
  Financial crises devastate Americans, destroying millions of jobs and businesses and leaving financial and economic scars for years after. *Solutionomics* details how to reduce the frequency and severity of financial crises, creating a more reliable source of consumer and company loans—the lifeblood of a growing economy.
- **Increasing Congressional Transparency and Accountability**
  Solutionomics outlines a four-step plan containing specific measures that would increase congressional transparency and accountability.

Are You Searching For…

Fresh approaches and new insights instead of the tired old ideas that got us to where we are today? Are you seeking solutions driven by return on investment instead of politics as usual and campaign donations? Are you longing for specific solutions instead of endless theoretical debates over economic ideologies? Are you tired of extreme, all or nothing ideas that pander to the most partisan elements of each political party? Do you instead want solutions that will allow America to both benefit from global trade and not be taken advantage of by other countries rather than having to choose between a trade war or continuing to be taken advantage? Do you believe there must be solutions that will benefit both companies and employees instead of pitting them against each other and demonizing one another? Do you want to reward the companies creating jobs in America and raising wages and end the policy of giving tax breaks to companies firing American employees? Do you think there must be a way to both ensure a stable source of the loans companies and consumers need and reduce the frequency and severity of financial crises? Then *Solutionomics* is the book for you.

2. *SOLUTIONOMICS* IS FOR YOU IF...

You simply want somebody to emphasize solutions, not political self-interest. You are discouraged and find yourself asking, "Is this all the better we can do?" or "Are these the only ideas we can come up with?" You have had enough of a Congress driven by political self-interest while global competitors drive American companies out of business.

You work hard every day contributing to the success and productivity of America but are fed up with the state of our politics and losing faith in the ability to achieve your financial goals. It is for the small business owner working to build his or her business in the face of competition from both larger, better-financed domestic competitors and global, state-owned enterprises subsidized by foreign governments. It is for the American companies and their employees increasingly threatened by global competitors playing by different rules.

Solutionomics is for the retirees who built this country and yet, are now left with having to choose between buying food or medicine this month as they wonder when their savings will run out.

It is for our veterans, those who sacrificed to keep America free, now having to wait months to finally receive care that is not equal to the sacrifice they made. These include my uncles who served honorably in World War II.

Solutionomics is for our youth, the future of our country. We have the responsibility to both show them that there is great opportunity for improvement and that it is achievable by outlining the specific solutions that would transform the opportunity into reality. They have the possibility to make the greatest impact of any generation in aligning congressional action with achieving America's economic potential. Where does this power come from? Social media. As a baby boomer said to me when discussing millennials, "They are a lot like we were with wanting to make the world a better place. The difference is that they have more than just three TV channels to work with." If they engage in the political process, the possibilities for improvement are endless because of the power of social media to increase congressional transparency and accountability.

Whether you long for Reagan's Morning in America, voted for Obama's Hope and Change, or to Make America Great Again, you have picked up the right book, because this book is about solutions, not politics.

3. HOW ARE YOU GOING TO REACT?

As you read the solutions outlined in the following pages you may think, "Congress will never do that." You may be right. *This* Congress may not implement some of the solutions. This doesn't mean the problem is the solutions; it means the problem is the members of Congress. Just like bad management in a company refusing to implement good ideas does not make the ideas bad, Congress' unwillingness to implement solutions does not mean the solutions are the problem. What it means is that perhaps it is time for new management, otherwise known as our Congress. With the right Congress, we can capitalize on the significant opportunity for improvement.

Don't get me wrong. I'm not naïve, thinking it will be easy. I'm also not going to passively accept the status quo and do nothing. This is a book about achievement, not giving up before trying just because it will require effort. That would not only be a missed opportunity, but it would be an affront both to our founding fathers who made the effort to overcome daunting odds to create the United States and the veterans who subsequently fought to defend the country they created. Are you going to be a part of helping America achieve its economic potential?

With the right Congress, we can capitalize on the significant opportunity for improvement.

Are you going to be a part of helping America achieve its economic potential?

Independent, Not Indebted

I do not work for a political party, lobbyist, PAC, or Super PAC—I am independent, not indebted. This allows me to evaluate policy solutions based on their return on investment to the American taxpayer, not a political agenda. I am also not part of the political establishment and, because of this, I am not restricted to the same old policy prescriptions Americans have been limited to for years.

> I do not work for a political party, lobbyist, PAC, or Super PAC—I am independent, not indebted.

I have not only studied and researched economics and finance, but I have also worked in the private sector. My experience is in the finance industry, evaluating a wide range of companies in a variety of sectors of the economy. It also includes working for Fortune 500 companies and small companies. This experience provides me with firsthand knowledge of how our economy works, including job creation and wage growth, a varied perspective on both large and small companies, and the way the finance sector operates as well as its role within the economy.

My political independence, educational background, and industry experience allow me to devise innovative solutions based on how our economy and finance system works and to evaluate them based on their return on investment to the American taxpayer, not a political agenda.

PART ONE

AND NOW FOR SOMETHING VERY DIFFERENT

4. SOLVE DIFFERENT™

Albert Einstein said, "We cannot solve our problems with the same thinking we used when we created them."
Apple said, "Think different."
At Solutionomics, *it's "Solve Different."*

Are you ready for something very different? Do you believe that the same old established approaches which created today's problems won't, all of a sudden, magically lead us to achieving America's economic potential? If so, then you're reading the right book, because *Solutionomics* looks at things very differently.

Achieving our economic potential requires a different approach. *Solutionomics* solves differently by focusing on return on investment (ROI), not political considerations. It also uses a different framework to analyze the source of our economic failings.

> *Solutionomics* solves differently by focusing on return on investment, not political considerations.

Neither poll-tested talking points nor vague campaign platitudes will lead America to achieving its economic potential. The extreme policy choices and narratives peddled by politicians and media pundits may fire up the "base," but they won't move us closer to achieving America's economic potential. What they do instead is discourage Americans, leaving them to ask in exasperation, "Is this the best we can do?" The answer is no. We can do better. And it begins by implementing an ROI-based approach to evaluating ideas.

Not Left, Not Right, ROI

Today's donor and lobbyist-driven political system and economic policies are literally bankrupting the U.S. and causing it to fall short of its immense potential.

Today's donor and lobbyist-driven political system and economic policies are literally bankrupting the U.S. and causing it to fall short of its immense potential.

Instead of political calculation, *Solutionomics* utilizes return on investment to evaluate which solutions will deliver the best result for the American taxpayer. It is only logical that, if Americans supply the majority of the money for government spending, the return on investment should be based on the return to the American taxpayer. This is very different from today's established system in which the spending of taxpayer dollars is based on campaign donations, lobbying dollars spent, and which special interest has more power. Implementing an ROI-based decision-making process is the first step in improving our economic and political systems.

Implementing an ROI-based decision-making process is the first step in improving our economic and political systems.

Solutionomics Solution #1: Implement an ROI-based decision-making process

5. USA INC.

How can the elements involved in achieving America's economic potential be untangled, organized, and analyzed? By viewing our economic and political systems as comprising an economic entity, USA Inc.

The idea of trying to analyze and improve our economic and political systems can be overwhelming. It can be like trying to untangle a massive ball of yarn comprised of multiple threads. Where do you start? Which string do you pull on? How do the threads relate to each other? It can be confusing, frustrating, and discouraging. It can make us long for the relative simplicity of a Gordian Knot. If that is not bad enough, when those who have not given up seek information and ideas for improving our economic or political systems, they are often confronted with conflicting information and self-serving rhetoric dished out from self-interested politicians, political party operatives, and paid pundits shilling for a special interest. Because of this, even earnest attempts to understand how to improve our economic and political systems can lead one to become more discouraged, disillusioned, and disengaged. But there is a way to make sense of it all—USA Inc.

USA Inc.

Solutionomics organizes the components of our political system into corporate equivalents. These include the United States'three branches of government, We the People, and the two major political parties—collectively comprising USA Inc.

The Founding Fathers of USA Inc.

The founding fathers created USA Inc. This was initiated through the Declaration of Independence and conceived through the U.S. Constitution. The Constitution is the equivalent of a company charter, containing the purpose, objectives, and structure governing USA Inc. The Constitution contains the purpose and principles that determine what the shareholders of USA Inc. believe in and the system they will live under. It represents USA Inc.'s values and governance structure. The Constitution contains the general guidelines and principles under which we have all agreed to live by.

Compliance department of USA Inc.—U.S. Supreme Court

Some companies have compliance departments. They make sure the company is following its rules and regulations and the law. USA Inc. needs to comply with the Constitution, the laws of the land, and regulations. Like most guidelines, their interpretation and implementation can be disputed. When this occurs, the judicial system and ultimately a group of nine citizens known as the United States Supreme Court, resolves specific disputes.

Shareholders of USA Inc.—We the People

The shareholders or owners of USA Inc. are We the People. They are supposed to be the beneficiaries of USA Inc. and take on its obligations, including debts.

CEO of USA Inc.—The President

USA Inc.'s CEO is the President of the United States. However, unlike a corporate CEO, the President's power is checked and balanced by the Supreme Court and managers of USA Inc.

Managers of USA Inc.—Congress

USA Inc.'s managers are the members of Congress. They are responsible for writing the specific laws that govern how USA Inc. will be run, including how taxes are assessed, how tax revenues are spent, the debt the country takes on, and in general, what can and can't be done. Congress is elected by the shareholders of USA Inc. However, much like in the case of corporations, who the shareholders get to vote for as its managers is largely determined by the Board of Directors and, as we will see, the choices shareholders get to vote for are often limited.

Board of Directors of USA Inc—Republicans and Democrats

In a corporation, the Board of Directors puts up individuals for election to manage the corporation. Similarly, USA Inc. has a Board of Directors that largely determines who is put up for election. Also, like some corporate Board of Directors, the Board of USA Inc. is divided, primarily, into two factions calling themselves the Democratic Party and the Republican Party. Because they have significant influence in determining who has the best chance of winning elections, the parties and their leaders wield significantly more power over USA Inc. than some may realize.

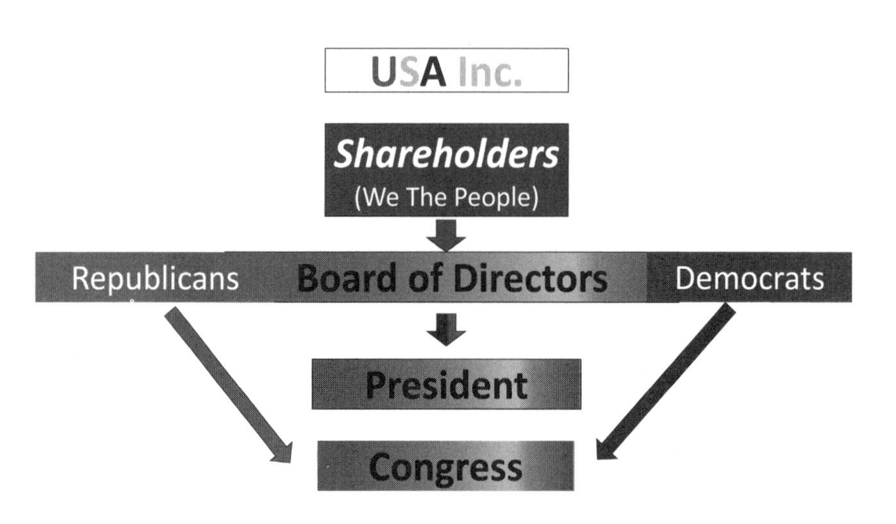

Something Very Dangerous Has Come Between Us

Notice that between the shareholders of USA Inc. and its managers is the Board of Directors and its two factions, the Republican and Democratic parties. The parties act as gatekeepers controlling who can viably run for political office. They make it exceedingly difficult for individuals to successfully run for office without their support, especially offices that require significant campaign dollars and volunteers, such as Congress. Anyone without their support will find it more difficult to make it to the halls of Congress. This stifles new ideas and ensures mediocrity, much like the effects of any monopoly. As a result, these factions are very powerful and certainly more powerful than is healthy for our country.

How big of a problem is this?

During the 2016 election cycle, multiple Democrats across the country challenging incumbent congressional Democrats were denied access to the Democratic National Committee's voter database, VoteBuilder.[2] Limiting challengers' access to this database hinders their efforts to fundraise, target voters, and unseat incumbents. Restricting access clearly goes against the principles of free and open competition, instead creating an environment favoring incumbents at the expense of challengers. This isn't just a problem within the Democratic Party, as Republican challengers have faced similar obstacles. This limits voter choice and would be the equivalent of two automakers or phone makers controlling the U.S. automobile or mobile device market, leaving consumers only two car or phone brands to choose from. If competition breeds the best outcomes, then small wonder why we have had such mediocre outcomes in Congress—there is limited competition. Two political parties largely determine who we get to vote for.

Two political parties largely determine who we get to vote for.

How Does USA Inc. Measure Profits? Jobs, Jobs, Jobs!

Traditional for-profit corporations exist to generate a financial profit for their shareholders. How does USA Inc. measure its "profits?" USA Inc.'s profits are good-paying jobs. The greater the number of better-paying jobs it

USA Inc.'s "profits" are good-paying jobs. USA Inc.'s primary economic objective is to increase the number of good-paying jobs and increase wages.

generates, the better its return on investment. USA Inc.'s primary economic goal is to increase the number of good-paying jobs and increase wages. Its "financial statements" measure jobs created, wage levels, and wage growth. Why jobs and wages?

Increasing the Number of Good-Paying Jobs and Wage Growth Are Keys to Overcoming Many Economic Shortcomings and Social Problems

Low wages and limited wage growth play a role in many economic issues facing USA Inc. Money may be the root of all evil, but the decline of good-paying jobs is the evil at the root of many of USA Inc.'s economic problems and contributes to many of its social problems.

Consider the following areas impacted by the creation or destruction of good-paying jobs:

Taxes: Increasing the number of good-paying jobs results in a larger income tax base, which allows for lowering tax rates without reducing tax revenue.

Deficits: Conversely, increasing good-paying jobs results in a larger income tax base, which would lead to greater tax revenues and can be used to pay down our deficit.

Economic Growth: With 70 percent of gross domestic product (GDP) coming from consumer purchases, increasing good-paying jobs leads to higher consumer income levels, increasing consumer purchasing power, which translates into increased consumer purchases and GDP growth.

Military Funding: Increased economic growth increases the funds available for military spending.

Corporate Revenues: Employed Americans earning good wages make the best customers. The more of them we have in the U.S., the more company revenues can increase.

Stock Market Valuations: Rising corporate revenues help to drive up stock values, providing better returns for investors and financial security for retirees.

Investment Opportunities: An increase in consumer purchasing power can increase demand for company products, increasing investment opportunities to meet the rising demand.

Social Security: Because each individual's Social Security payment and the government's ability to make the payments is based on each individual's earnings, the more people earn, the greater their Social Security payment.

Welfare Expenditures: Increased employment at higher wages increases income levels. As a result, fewer people would qualify for welfare, including Medicaid, Supplemental Nutrition Assistance, subsidized housing, and home heating assistance, among others.

Expanding the Middle Class: The higher the percentage of USA Inc.'s population working in good-paying jobs, the greater the economic output potential, leading to the possibility of greater economic prosperity. Increasing good-paying jobs would create greater incentives to work, increasing labor force participation and economic growth.

Home Values: The value of an asset is determined not only by the supply of the asset but also the purchasing power of the buyers. Increasing good-paying jobs results in more people being able to buy homes, resulting in increasing home values.

Education Funding: Property taxes are a significant source of education funding. Increasing home values would increase property tax revenues, making more funds available for education funding.

Property Taxes: Rising home values would allow property tax rates to be reduced while generating the same level of revenue.

Financial System Stability: An increase in the number of good-paying jobs means more prime home buyers, prime credit card borrowers, and prime automobile borrowers, reducing the need to make loans to subprime borrowers, as there would be more prime borrowers and fewer subprime borrowers. Aggressive lending to subprime home buyers was the spark that ignited the recent financial meltdown and economic collapse. What if we took away the spark and kindling that nearly burned down the financial house, replacing it with more buyers who could make the payments?

Incarceration: It is much better to have someone working a good-paying job and adding to the productive capacity of USA Inc. than to have them sitting in prisons.

Division and Polarization: Good-paying jobs would increase feelings of financial security. This is critical because the opposite—feelings of personal financial insecurity—result in people turning on each other as they look for a cause of their financial insecurity. This turning against each other weakens USA Inc., much like when teammates turn against each other during a game. They are less competitive.

What Does USA Inc. "Sell"?

Corporations sell products and/or services for financial profit. If good-paying jobs are the profit we seek, what does USA Inc. sell in return? USA Inc. has many items of value that it "sells." This is our first "aha moment," or, to use a business consulting term, paradigm shift.

USA Inc. Has Items of Great Value to "Sell"

The first and most valuable item USA Inc. has to "sell" is access to its highly lucrative market. And you are part of creating this highly valuable market every day through your purchases. No country or economic union is a more important market to companies than USA Inc., and you, the shareholders of USA Inc., create this market every day through your purchases.

The first and most valuable item USA Inc. has to "sell" is access to its highly lucrative market

Stop Begging and Start Negotiating!

USA Inc.'s CEOs and managers should be maximizing the return on investment received from granting access to the lucrative American consumer or, at least, achieving returns equal to those the leaders of other countries are earning in return for access to their markets. How far behind are we? The Chinese government has required companies wanting to sell products in China to partner with local firms and manufacture the goods in China. It has required technology transfers from companies that want to sell their products to Chinese consumers. Now, that's negotiating. Meanwhile, we trip over ourselves begging companies to stay in the U.S. Why are we doing this? We have a highly desirable market. While China requires companies wanting to sell their products to the Chinese consumer to both manufacture in China and transfer

> While China requires companies wanting to sell their products to the Chinese consumer to both manufacture in China and transfer technology, we are throwing money at companies begging them to stay in the U.S.—I want China's negotiators!

technology, we are throwing money at companies begging them to stay in the U.S.—I want China's negotiators!

Who Are USA Inc.'s Customers?

Before we list some of the other valuable "products" USA Inc. has to offer, we need to identify the "buyers," the "customers" of USA Inc. Who are these customers wanting access to the U.S. market? They are corporations. They want and *need* access to the United States consumer. It is what all of USA Inc.'s customers want access to. Yet, we always seem to be begging or cajoling companies to operate here. Really? We possess one of the most valuable assets in the world and that is the best our management team can do? Companies have executives negotiating on behalf of their shareholders, as they should, but who is negotiating on behalf of the interests of USA Inc.'s shareholders? Members of Congress are paid to, but it often seems they are negotiating more on behalf of their personal political interests. The problem isn't companies trying to get the best deals for their shareholders; it is

> The problem isn't companies trying to get the best deals for their shareholders; it is members of Congress trying to get the best deals for themselves, not the shareholders of USA Inc.

members of Congress trying to get the best deals for themselves, not the shareholders of USA Inc.

What Else Does USA Inc. "Sell?"

In addition to the sheer size and affluence of the American market, USA Inc. has many other assets which make the U.S. the most desirable market in the world. First, USA Inc. offers the legal protection that comes from operating within the U.S. This includes the laws, courts, and enforcement that are the backbone of USA Inc.'s legal system. Customers of USA Inc. also benefit from the transparency of the legal system, its stability, and relative predictability. For some of its customers, the most valuable benefit of our legal system is the protection of intellectual property that comes from our patent system and laws. In today's increasingly unstable world, USA Inc. offers an unmatched and increasingly valuable "product:" social stability. USA Inc. customers seek the certainty that mob rule or rule by force will not overtake the country. They also value that the government is not subject to unexpected, nondemocratic military changes of leadership. The presidents and managers of USA Inc. are not regularly deposed or subject to mob rule. Instead, USA Inc. offers the certainty that property rights will be protected, property will be protected, and that USA Inc.'s government is insulated from small groups using violent means to take control. The value of this social stability increases as the social stability of other countries decreases. When occurrences of violent protests around the world and nationalization of private corporations' assets increase, the value of the relative social stability offered by USA Inc. increases further. USA Inc. also offers relatively low crime rates. Unlike in some countries, operating in the U.S. doesn't require private, military-style security forces guarding facilities. Security guards for company employees aren't required as they travel throughout the U.S. Additionally, trucks, airplanes, and trains carrying goods can move freely throughout the United States without fear of attack or being subjected to extortion. It's the best of both worlds for the customers of USA Inc. Not only do we not nationalize corporations, but when the largest corporations experience financial duress, sometimes we bail them out! We throw them a lifeline, and when they are resuscitated, we release them back into the wild.

Giving them the benefit of the doubt, perhaps our managers, members of Congress, just aren't aware of the incredible value of what USA Inc. offers its customers. Or maybe it is that some in Congress instead spend most of their time seeking the campaign contributions *they* need rather than seeking the best deals for the shareholders of USA Inc. Even in the case of the dedicated members of Congress who are begging and cajoling corporations to create more jobs, I have just one question: Why are you begging? Why aren't you negotiating? This is one of, if not the most important, shifts in mindset that must occur if we are to secure a better return on our investment for the shareholders of USA Inc. Getting a better return on investment requires leveraging the assets USA Inc. has to offer. It is the second solution in increasing the number of higher-paying jobs.

***Solutionomics* Solution #2: USA Inc. managers start negotiating from a position of strength, a strength that is derived by the simple fact that, along with many other assets, we have a highly desirable asset: Access to the U.S. consumer**.

It is the least they can do on behalf of you, the shareholders of USA Inc., who create this market every day through your purchases. They should be driving better deals…on behalf of its shareholders. How we get Congress to do this is covered in Part II, Section V, titled, "*Increasing Congressional Transparency and Accountability.*"

PART TWO

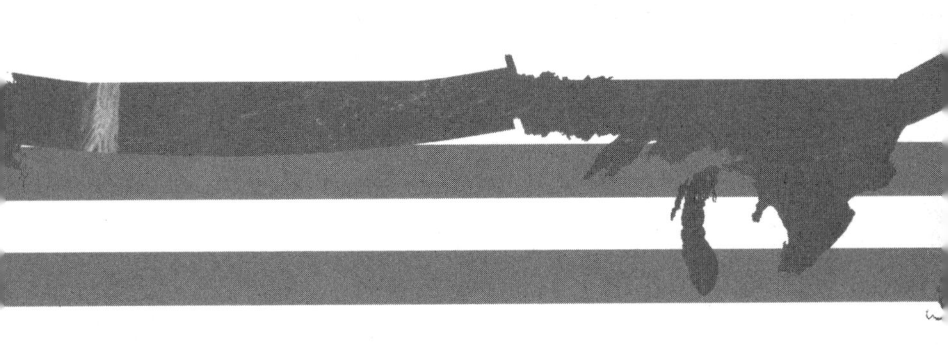

SOLUTIONS

SECTION I

CREATING AN INCENTIVE-BASED CORPORATE TAX POLICY

6. HOPE IS NOT A TAX POLICY

Corporate tax policy is the most obvious area where implementing ROI in evaluating economic policies can make a significant difference. A truly incentive-based corporate tax policy based on maximizing ROI would create more jobs and increase wages at a lower cost to taxpayers. This would be in contrast to what Congress has done for many years: cut corporate tax rates and hope wages and jobs increase. The December 2017 Tax Cuts and Jobs Act (TCJA) was more of the same. In it, Congress handed out universal and, most importantly, *unconditional* tax cuts without any requirements

> Congress, in effect, said to companies, "Fire Americans, no problem. Your tax rate will go down like every other corporation. Reduce wages, also no problem. Your tax rate will go down."

for companies to increase wages, jobs, or business investment—Congress simply continued to hope that companies would raise wages, hire more, and increase business investment. Congress, in effect, said to companies, "Fire Americans, no problem. Your tax rate will go down like every other corporation. Reduce wages, also no problem. Your tax rate will go down." Corporate tax policy is the single greatest opportunity for improvement through ROI-based policy decision-making.

7. CORPORATE TAX CUT RHETORIC VS. REALITY

TCJA's Dismal ROI

The first step in estimating the ROI is calculating the investment or cost. According to estimates from the Congressional Budget Office,[1] the TCJA will add $1.9 trillion in additional debt from 2018-2028. Importantly, that includes the estimated positive economic effects on the economy and increased tax revenue—or what is sometimes referred to as "dynamic budgeting." $1.9 trillion is a massive investment that can only be justified by a massive return on investment. Unfortunately, it looks like We the People aren't even going to make their investment back, let alone a return on their investment. Think about that: You, your children, and grandchildren are going to owe $1.9 trillion more. And for what?

Wage Growth Woes

A key justification for the TCJA heaping an estimated $1.9 trillion of additional debt on We the People was the promise of

1 Ibid.

substantial wage hikes. These promises were made by President Trump's Council of Economic Advisers on the White House's website in a document titled "Corporate Tax Reform and Wages: Theory and Evidence":

> *"Reducing the statutory federal corporate tax rate from 35 to 20 percent would, the analysis below suggests, increase average household income in the United States by,* very conservatively, $4,000 *annually."*

The document goes on to say:

> *"When we use the more optimistic estimates from the literature,* wage boosts are over $9,000 *for the average U.S. household."*

Then-House Speaker Paul Ryan's website also promoted the Council of Economic Advisers' report, claiming that, on average, the proposed corporate tax cuts would result in at least a $4,000 annual increase in wages.

Were these promises of meteoric wage growth kept? Not even close.

During the twelve-month period following passage of the tax bill, from December 2017 to December 2018, average hourly wages grew $0.84 per hour.[2] During the twelve-month period prior to passage of the tax bill, wages grew $0.69 per hour.[3] So, during the twelve months after the tax bill was passed, wage growth grew

---

2 U.S. Bureau of Labor Statistics.

3 Ibid.

only $0.15 per hour[4] more than the twelve months prior to the tax bill being passed, not exactly a wage bonanza.

	12 Months *Before* TCJA	12 Months *After* TCJA	Difference
Annual Wage Increase	$.69/Hour	$.84/Hour	$.15/Hour

Source: **Solutionomics** *calculations using U.S. Bureau of Labor Statistics data*

In the twelve months after the TCJA was passed the rate of wage growth increased $300! Not exactly the $4,000 to $9,000 promised.

For a person working forty hours a week and fifty weeks a year, the $0.15 increase in wage growth versus 2017's wage growth equates to a whopping $300-a-year increase. That's right, in the twelve months after the TCJA was passed, the rate of wage growth increased $300! Not exactly the $4,000 to $9,000 promised.

Looking at inflation-adjusted wage growth shows an even bleaker picture. During the twelve months after the passage of the tax bill, from December 2017 to December 2018, inflation-adjusted

4 Ibid.

wage growth was less than 1 percent, 0.8 percent to be exact.[5] While that is a staggeringly low number, it looks even worse when one considers that inflation-adjusted wage growth for the twelve months prior to passage of the tax bill was 0.7 percent, nearly the same.[6] It is disingenuous to pretend that the difference in wage growth before and after the recently passed tax bill is anything other than disappointing and much less than what was promised. What happened?

	12 Months *Before* TCJA	12 Months *After* TCJA	Difference
Annual Wage Increase (%)	.8%	.7%	.1%

Source: **Solutionomics** *calculations using U.S. Bureau of Labor Statistics data*

First, the campaign to gain support for corporate tax cuts required outlandish promises, including wage gains ranging from $4,000-$9,000: There was no way that was going to happen. The current average hourly wage of $27.16[7] equates to $54,960 per year. The $4,000 and $9,000 promised wage hikes would have required between a 7.2 percent and 16.4 percent wage increase. When's the

5 Ibid.

6 Ibid.

7 Ibid.

last time you received that type of raise? Most are lucky if they get a raise that keeps up with inflation.

Second, wages are determined by leverage between employers and employees, not tax cuts. Significant increases in corporate after-tax profits won't increase wages if employers have the negotiating power. Wage growth is a function of both what companies *can* pay and what they *must* pay.

> Wage growth is a function of both what companies *can* pay and what they *must* pay.

Wage growth requires profitable companies that have the money to increase wages *and* employees having the leverage necessary to negotiate wage increases. No matter how much corporate tax rates are cut and company profits increase, they won't increase wages if they have the leverage. In the end, rising corporate profits without rising employee negotiating power will not increase the pace of wage growth. While the promised $4,000-$9,000 wage increases sounded good and people wanted it to be true, reality often differs from the promises made by politicians.

> While the promised $4,000-$9,000 wage increases sounded good and people wanted it to be true, reality often differs from the promises made by politicians.

Business Investment Declines Explained

If all the money companies saved in taxes didn't go into wage increases, where did it go? Maybe it went into significantly greater rates of business investment growth? Not according to a January 2019 National Association for Business Economics survey of respondents representing various companies and industries. Eighty-four percent of those responding to the survey indicated that the TCJA had no impact on their investment or hiring plans[10]and true to their word, growth in business investment largely remained flat subsequent to passage of the TCJA.

During the first twelve months following passage of the tax bill, fixed business investment (on an inflation-adjusted basis) increased $155 billion,[8] which sounds good. However, during the twelve months before the TCJA was passed, business investment increased $173 billion[9], $18 billion more. That's right, fixed business investment growth was lower after the TCJA was passed. Not exactly what was promised.

Growth in equipment investment also declined after passage of the TCJA, falling 34 percent.

Growth in equipment investment also declined after passage of the TCJA, falling 34 percent. During the twelve months after the TCJA was passed, equipment investment increased $71 billion, down significantly from the $101 billion increase experienced in the twelve months before passage of the TCJA.[10]

Given that that tax bill provided for 100 percent and immediate deductibility of capital investments, why did the rate of

8 Bureau of Economic Analysis

9 Ibid.

10 Ibid.

growth in equipment investment decline as opposed to increase? Simple. Customer demand is the primary driver of business investment, not tax rates.

Think about it. If you owned a business and your tax rate was cut but demand for your products remained the same, would you increase investment? Of course not. It would be the equivalent of a CEO doubling his company's production capacity when sales orders were little changed and, when asked by the board of directors why production capacity was doubled, saying, "Because the tax rate was reduced."

While tax rates can influence *where* investments in production occur, it is secondary to demand when determining *whether* to increase investment. Clearly, businesses so far have not seen the demand necessary to increase the business investment growth rate.

While tax rates can influence *where* investments in production occur, it is secondary to demand when determining *whether* to increase investment.

Even if the pace of business investment does increase, it may not be all it is cracked up to be. Why? There are no requirements for the equipment that companies purchase to be made in America. This means a company can buy equipment produced outside the U.S., generating jobs outside the U.S., and still receive full tax benefits despite buying foreign-made equipment—and, as we will see, this is a very real possibility in today's world.

Additionally, businesses now have less of an incentive to increase investment in the U.S., thanks to the TCJA. For all the talk of encouraging American jobs and manufacturing, the TCJA eliminated the Domestic Production Activities Deduction. This deduction was intended to reward manufacturers for producing goods domestically, as opposed to overseas, through favorable tax treatment of income related to domestically produced goods. If the goal of the TCJA was to increase American jobs and encourage domestic manufacturing, why did they eliminate this? Because the TCJA desperately needed to find money in the tax code to offset its massive reduction of the corporate tax rate from 35 percent to 21 percent. Congress traded a tax deduction that created an incentive for companies to produce in the U.S. with a tax cut that does not consider whether companies increase production and hiring in the U.S. The phrase, "Watch what I do, not what I say," comes to mind.

Congress traded a tax deduction that created an incentive for companies to produce in the U.S. with a tax cut that does not consider whether companies increase production and hiring in the U.S.

Some may argue that eliminating this tax break specifically designed to increase production in the U.S.is okay because companies will receive a much bigger incentive via reducing the statutory rate from 35 percent to 21 percent. Why? There is nothing in the TCJA that ties the reduction to domestic production. Rather, companies can reduce production in the U.S., and

Companies can reduce production in the U.S., and they will still see their tax rate nearly cut in half. That's not an incentive; that's policy ineptitude they will still see their tax rate nearly cut in half. That's not an incentive; that's policy ineptitude.

U.S. Taxpayers Subsidizing Japanese and German Jobs

The TCJA will likely end up subsidizing the purchase of foreign-made robotics.

The TCJA will likely end up subsidizing the purchase of foreign-made robotics. The TCJA provides for full and immediate expensing of equipment purchases. The idea was that it would encourage companies to invest more in equipment, creating American jobs. The reality, however, may be something very different. This is because there is no requirement for the equipment to be produced in the U.S. Companies can buy equipment made in Japan, Germany, or anywhere else and receive the full and immediate expensing—so much for the taxpayer's ROI on that tax incentive.

According to *The Wall Street Journal*, in 1995, 81 percent of U.S. industrial production equipment was American-made; today, it is only 19 percent.[11]

As an example, Tesla uses German and Japanese industrial robots, not American equipment.[12] In 2016, Japan and Germany alone accounted for more than 50 percent of total industrial robot exports, with the U.S. accounting for only 4.3 percent.[13]

11 Daniel Michaels, "Foreign Robots Invade American Factory Floors," *The Wall Street Journal*, March 26, 2017.

12 "Robotic Stocks That Could Profit From Tesla's Model 3 Ramp-Up (and Beyond)," Madison.com, Jan. 21, 2018.

13 *WorldsTopExports.com*.

The U.S. just isn't as dominant in robotics as some might think. Nine out of the ten largest industrial robot manufacturers by industrial sales volume were based outside the U.S.[14] Yet, under the TCJA, companies benefit from full and immediate expensing of purchases of foreign-produced equipment, with no benefit to American workers.

in 1995, 81 percent of U.S. industrial production equipment was American made; today, it is only 19 percent

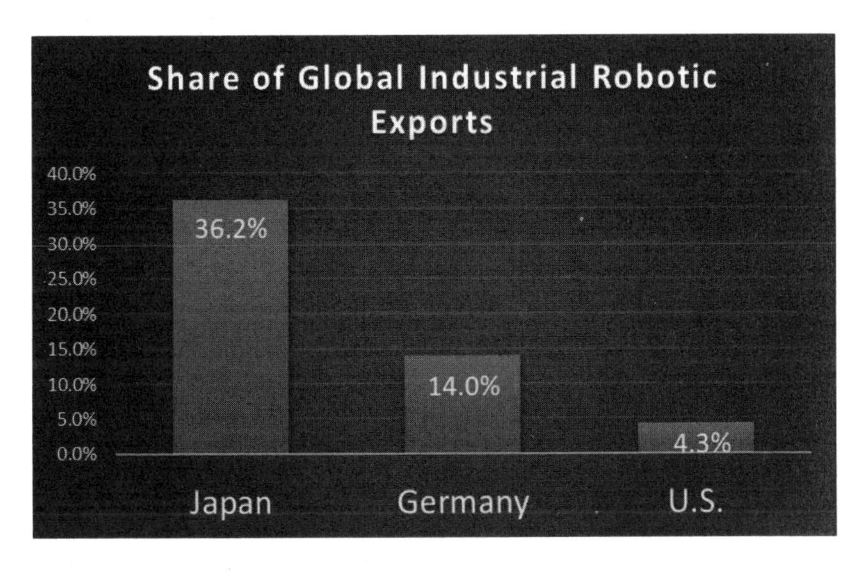

Source: **Solutionomics,** *using data from WorldsTopExports.com.*

14 "Major Companies in the Global Industrial Robot Market in 2017, by Revenue (in Billion U.S. Dollars)," Statista.com, https://www.statista.com/statistics/317178/leading-industrial-robot-companies-globally-by-revenue/.

Machines Over Man

Well, at least we are narrowing down where all the company tax cuts went. We know company tax savings didn't go to significantly increasing wages or business investment. That leaves hiring. Surely companies took their significant tax savings and hired millions of additional American workers? While that was what was sold to the American people, unfortunately for them, that is not what happened.

During the twelve months after passage of the TCJA, 2,674,000[15] jobs were added to the American economy. Sounds impressive until you realize that, during the twelve months before passage of the TCJA, the American economy added 2,153,000.[16] That's right, in return for taking on $1.9 trillion in estimated additional debt, the American people received a little over 500,000 more jobs. That equates to a cost of more than $3,646,833 per job! That is not a good return on investment. For $1.9 trillion, We the People should be getting a lot more. How much more? Previously, we saw that the average wage of $27.16 equated to about $55,000 per year. For the $1.9 trillion in additional debt levied on We the People, we could have paid

> For the $1.9 trillion in additional debt levied on We the People, we could have paid 3,454,545 people $55,000 a year for ten years, not the 521,000 jobs created, jobs that, thanks to the TCJA, can be eliminated next year and companies will still pay the same lower tax rate.

15 U.S. Bureau of Labor Statistics.

16 Ibid.

3,454,545 people $55,000 a year for ten years, not the 521,000 jobs created, jobs that, thanks to the TCJA, can be eliminated next year and companies will still pay the same lower tax rate.

Not only did the promised hiring bonanza never occur, before the ink even dried on the TCJA, companies instead fired Americans, all thanks to our Congress' incompetence, which allowed companies to receive tax cuts even if they fired Americans. In what may be the most ironic tax-cut-related round of layoffs, and likely surprising twist to the architects of the TCJA, Kimberly-Clark not only said it was going to eliminate up to 5,500 jobs but that the tax savings from the TCJA would be used to fund the layoffs.[17] While AT&T announced at least 4,000 job cuts,[18] in the granddaddy of them all, Verizon is laying off 44,000 workers and transferring 2,500 call center jobs to India.[19] Walmart announced layoffs

Not only did the promised hiring bonanza never occur, before the ink even dried on the TCJA, companies instead fired Americans, all thanks to our Congress' incompetence, which allowed companies to receive tax cuts even if they fired Americans.

17 Kate Taylor, "The Maker of Huggies and Kleenex Is Firing Up to 5,500 Workers—and It's Using Trump Tax Cuts to Pay for the Layoffs," *Business Insider*, Jan. 25, 2018

18 Eric Schaal, "These Companies Laid Off Large Numbers of Employees After Taking Trump's Tax Cuts," *The Cheat Sheet*, July 11, 2018.

19 Jean Baptiste Su, "Verizon Lays Off 44,000, Transfers 2,500 More IT Jobs to Indian Outsourcer Infosys," *Forbes*, Oct. 5, 2018.

of nearly 10,000 employees[20] shortly after passage of the TCJA. Remember the Indiana-based heating and air conditioning maker Carrier Corporation that received more than $7 million in tax breaks from the state of Indiana? It didn't take Carrier long to lay off more than 200 workers[21] after the TCJA was passed. Not to be outdone, the American icon Harley-Davidson announced it would be closing its Kansas City, Missouri, plant, laying off approximately 800 workers.[22] Macy's announced it would be laying off 5,000[23] workers while Tenet Healthcare announced it would lay off 2,000 workers.[24] As part of a restructuring plan Hewlett-Packard announced up to 5,000 job cuts,[25] while in the financial industry, despite reaping significant tax-cut-related profits, Wells Fargo announced it would lay off 26,500[26] employees and Citibank announced that it could eliminate half of its 20,000 technology and operations staff, driven primarily by

---

20 Jackie Wattles and Ben Geier, "63 Sam's Club Stores Are Closing Their Doors," *CNNMoney*, Jan. 11, 2018.

21 Chris Isidore, "Carrier Plant Trump Pledged to Save Lays Off Another 215 Workers," *CNNMoney*, Jan. 11, 2018.

22 Robert A. Cronkleton and Mike Hendricks, "About 800 Workers to Lose Jobs as Harley-Davidson Closes Its Kansas City Assembly Plant," *The Kansas City Star*, Jan. 30, 2018.

23 Nathan Bomey, "Macy's Announces 5,000 Job Cuts, 7 New Store Closures," *USA Today*, Jan. 4, 2018.

24 Korri Kezar, "Tenet Healthcare Now Expects to Lay Off 2,000 Workers," *Dallas Business Journal*, Jan. 9, 2018.

25 "HP Sees Up to 5,000 Job Cuts as Part of Restructuring Plan," Reuters, June 5, 2018.

26 Kevin Wack, "Wells Fargo to Cut Up to 26,000 Jobs Within Three Years," *American Banker*, Sept. 20, 2018.

automation.[27] Citigroup's announcement should come as no surprise, given that the TCJA's Machines Over Man tax policy gave no tax incentives for hiring humans, while allowing companies to immediately deduct 100 percent of the cost of equipment purchases. In a move that will directly affect Americans suffering from Alzheimer's and Parkinson's, after receiving its massive corporate tax cuts, Pfizer announced it would be ending funding for its Alzheimer's and Parkinson's research and development, including laying off nearly 300 scientists.[28] In June 2018, Tesla announced that it would be laying off 9 percent of its workforce.[29] Finally, despite both a massive bailout that cost Americans $11.2 billion and significant tax cuts, General Motors announced 14,000 layoffs.[30]

This list shows two very important facts. First, companies make hiring and firing decisions based on several factors beyond tax rates including the following:

1. Customer demand. Adam Smith knew this, stating, "Unless the demand is such to afford the builder his profit…he will build no more houses."[31]

---

27 Laura Noonan, "Citibank Issues Stark Warning on Automation of Bank Jobs," *Financial Times*, June 11, 2018.

28 "Pfizer Ends Research for New Alzheimer's, Parkinson's Drugs," Reuters, Jan. 7, 2018.

29 Claudia Assis, "Tesla to Lay Off 9% of Its Workforce, Elon Musk Says," *MarketWatch*, June 12, 2018.

30 Tom Krisher, "GM to Slash Up to 14,000 Jobs in North America; 7 Plants Could Close as Part of Restructuring," Associated Press, Nov. 26, 2018.

31 Adam Smith, *The Wealth of Nations* (Chicago: University of Chicago Press, 1976), Volume II, Book IV, 390

2. Automation. This allows companies to replace people with technology. The trend of automation was only exacerbated by the TCJA, as it favored machines over man.
3. CEO compensation. If a company's stock price isn't going up fast enough for Wall Street, it can cause the CEO, whose compensation is tied to stock performance, to fire Americans despite receiving substantial tax cuts.

Second, the TCJA was based on a Machines Over Man tax policy, even in the face of growing fears of automation eliminating millions of jobs. While companies were directly incentivized to buy more equipment through 100 percent and immediate deductibility of equipment purchases, even if foreign-made, there were no such direct incentives for hiring people. Congress, in effect, encouraged automating and eliminating more jobs.

> Companies make hiring and firing decisions based on customer demand, not tax rates. Adam Smith knew this, stating, "Unless the demand is such to afford the builder his profit...he will build no more houses."

> The TCJA was based on a Machines Over Man tax policy, which favors machines over man, even in the face of growing fears of automation eliminating millions of jobs.

Of Dividends, Deficits and Stock Buybacks

Wages didn't increase as promised. The rate of business investment growth declined. Employment growth didn't skyrocket as promised. Where did the money saved from the corporate tax cuts go? Surprise, surprise—dividends and stock buybacks. Just how many stock buybacks are we talking about? Hundreds of billions.

Apple alone announced $100 billion in stock buybacks on top of its $23.5 billion in first-quarter 2018 stock buybacks.[32] Remember the previously mentioned Harley-Davidson, Wells Fargo, Verizon, and Pfizer job cuts? Well, Harley-Davidson announced $700 million in share buybacks shortly after it said it would close its Kansas City plant.[33] Wells Fargo is expected to lay off 26,500 workers and yet, in what would be a record for banks, was planning to hand out $32.8 billion in stock buybacks and dividends.[34] After committing to $10 billion in dividend payout obligations,[35] Verizon apparently did not have enough money, so they had to cut 44,000 employees. And while Pfizer seemingly didn't have enough money to continue their Alzheimer's and Parkinson's research, they did have enough money to buy back $10 billion worth of stock.[36]

JPMorgan Chase estimated that firms would buy back at least $800 billion in shares in 2018.[37] Not only is that an astounding

32 Stephen Nellis, "Apple Surprises With Solid iPhone Sales, Announces $100 Billion Buyback," Reuters, May 1, 2018.

33 Kate Gibson, "Harley-Davidson Cut Jobs, Repurchased Shares After Tax Cut," CBS News, May 23, 2018.

34 "Wells Fargo's $33 Billion Capital Return Plan Is a New Record for U.S. Banks," *Forbes*, July 5, 2018

35 "Verizon: Near Perfect Dividend Hike," *Seeking Alpha*, Sept. 11, 2018.

36 "Pfizer Announces New $10 Billion Share Buyback, Hikes Dividend," Reuters, Dec. 18, 2017.

37 Jeff Cox, "Companies Projected to Use Tax Cut Windfall for Record Share Buyback, JP Morgan Says," CNBC, March 2, 2018.

amount of money going to stock buybacks instead of wage growth or business investment, it's 51 percent more than in 2017.[38] Add in dividends and S&P Dow Jones Indices analyst Howard Silverblatt estimated that, when looking at both share buybacks and dividends, they may reach $1 trillion in 2018[39]—a record.

So tax reform was passed, and share buybacks are now expected to increase 51 percent. It sure would have been nice if, instead, wage growth and business investment increased 51 percent in 2018. However, we got a new sales job extolling the virtues of share buybacks to justify the TCJA's $1.9 trillion in additional debt to be placed on We the People.

Yeah, Yeah, That's It. Stock Buybacks Are Good for Americans!

What do you do when wages didn't increase as promised, business investment growth declined, and employment growth didn't skyrocket as promised? Change the sales pitch. While share buybacks weren't part of the original TCJA sales pitch, they magically became an after-the-fact justification for the tax cuts and massive additional debt caused by the tax cuts. In the May 15, 2018 edition of "Tax Facts Tuesday" put out by the majority in control of the House Committee on Ways and Means, stock buybacks were trumpeted as something every American should be grateful for. The document title sums up the abrupt change in sales job, "Stock Buybacks and Investment: Good News for American Workers."

38 Ibid.

39 Noel Randewich, "S&P 500 Companies Return $1 Trillion to Shareholders in Tax-Cut Surge," Reuters, May 25, 2018.

I guess I'd also be forced to sell stock buybacks if the promised wage growth, increased business investment, and skyrocketing job growth promised didn't occur. My comments are not a commentary on the merits or shortcomings of stock buybacks. They are a commentary on the fact that stock buybacks weren't what we were promised if we cut the corporate tax rate.

Stock Buybacks Are a Symptom of the Problem, Not the Problem Itself

Some have argued for limiting stock buybacks. That won't solve the problem because stock buybacks aren't the problem, they are a symptom of the problem—two problems, actually. The first problem is the highly flawed TCJA. It had no requirements for companies to increase hiring or wages to receive tax cuts. I don't blame companies for the stock buybacks; I blame Congress for writing a flawed tax bill.

While the TCJA could be fixed through legislation, the second problem is more intractable and of greater consequence to USA Inc. achieving its economic potential. The reason companies plowed hundreds of billions of dollars into stock buybacks is simple: some companies received more cash from the tax cuts than they knew what to do with. They ended up with more cash than they had good investment opportunities, so they plowed their tax cuts into buybacks. *That* is the primary problem—companies didn't have enough growth opportunities relative to their after-tax earnings. It is not surprising that companies would increase stock buybacks. What else were they going to do with the excess cash? Stock buybacks, in general, will increase when companies run out of good investment opportunities. The stock buybacks confirm that some companies didn't need more cash; they needed more customers. The TCJA missed the opportunity to create more demand for companies' products, instead creating a glut of cash, at least for some companies.

> The stock buybacks confirm that some companies didn't need more cash; they needed more customers. The TCJA missed the opportunity to create more demand for companies.

8. CONGRESS, NOT CORPORATE AMERICA, IS THE CULPRIT

If you feel outrage over a slew of companies increasing share buybacks and some even firing Americans after receiving massive tax cuts, don't vilify the companies, vote to change Congress.

While it is insulting to be promised massive wage increases if we cut the corporate tax rate, only to cut the corporate tax rate and, instead, see a tsunami of company share buybacks, consider who made it all possible: Congress. Or, if you are dismayed that company tax rates were slashed, and companies didn't generate the promised jobs, remember that, thanks to Congress, companies were under no obligation to increase hiring to receive lower tax rates. Why am I repeatedly making this point? Because it is only through accurately focusing on the source of the recent corporate tax cut failure—Congress—and expressing your views by voting, attending town halls, and organizing get-out-the-vote drives

> Thanks to Congress, companies were under no obligation to increase hiring to receive lower tax rates.

that anything will change. If you think handing out unconditional corporate tax cuts like candy is poor management on behalf of the shareholders of USA Inc., then vote against those who voted for the bill.

Congress Put Donors Over Voters

What makes this worse is that Congress should have seen this coming from a mile away. Before the tax bill was passed, 46 percent of companies surveyed by Bank of America Merrill Lynch said they would increase share buybacks. This compares to only 35 percent saying they would use the extra cash on capital expenditures.[40] Worse still, in an ominous sign that should have not been ignored, when the audience was asked during a *Wall Street Journal* CEO Council event how many CEOs would use increased after-tax earnings to bolster investment, only a few hands were raised. This prompted National Economic Council Director Gary Cohn to ask, "Why aren't the other hands up?"[41] No one should have

Before the tax bill was passed, 46 percent of companies surveyed by Bank of America Merrill Lynch said they would increase share buybacks.

40 Jonathan Garber, "Here's What America's Biggest Companies Plan to Do With All That Cash Coming Back to the U.S.," *Business Insider*, Dec. 20, 2017.

41 Tucker Higgins, "CEOs Raise Doubts About Gary Cohn's Top Argument for Cutting the Corporate Tax Rate Right in Front of Him," CNBC, Nov. 15, 2017.

been surprised by the parade of share buyback announcements after passage of the TCJA.

So why, in the face of the Bank of America survey results and limited CEO commitment to increasing investment, did our esteemed managers known as Congress pass corporate tax cuts? That's right, because of campaign donations. Senator Lindsey Graham (R-SC) and Representative Chris Collins (R-NY) came right out and said so.

> *Q: What happens if the GOP isn't able to pass tax reform?*
>
> *Graham: "The party fractures, most incumbents in 2018 will get a severe primary challenge, a lot of them will probably lose, the base will fracture, the financial contributions will stop. Other than that it'll be fine!"*[42]

Responding to a reporter asking about tax reform, Collins replied:

> *"My donors are basically saying, 'Get it done or don't ever call me again.' "*[43]

---

42 Lauren Fox, "Hill Republican Dilemma: Dash to Pass Cash or Face Donor Backlash," CNN, Nov. 13, 2017.

43 Ibid.

9. THE CORPORATE TAX RATE DOES NOT MATTER AS MUCH AS...

Basing each company's tax rate on its wage levels, wage growth, and job creation...in America, that is how to achieve a better return on investment for the shareholders of USA Inc.

After comparing the tax cut rhetoric to the sobering reality, some have called for rolling back the corporate tax cuts. Conversely, others think we need to lower corporate tax rates further, calling for what they label "Tax Reform 2.0." They are both missing the point: The corporate tax rate does not matter...as much as tying company tax rates to what the shareholders of USA Inc. want and need—greater wage and job growth. The TCJA missed an obvious opportunity to leverage companies' focus on earnings growth to create more jobs and wage growth by giving companies the opportunity to grow their after-tax earnings *if* they increase hiring and wages.

> The TCJA missed an obvious opportunity to leverage companies' need for earnings growth to create more jobs and wage growth by giving companies the opportunity to grow their after-tax earnings *if* they increase hiring and wages.

Calls to raise or lower the corporate tax rate are merely rehashing the same old tax debates, based on the same old conflicting views of the effects of cutting corporate tax rates. Rather than basing policy on outdated ideological debates, it is time we implement a policy that ties corporate tax cuts to results.

We need a result-based corporate tax code. We need to finally tie corporate tax rates to wage levels, wage growth, and job creation. It is the opposite of the irresponsible and naïve hope-based corporate tax policy we have had. It is also the opposite of merely increasing tax rates with no direct connection to wage or job growth. Making corporate tax cuts contingent on job and wage growth would provide a true incentive to raise wages and increase hiring. That is how you get a better return on investment for the shareholders of USA Inc. It is also how you bridge the divide between Republicans' belief that tax cuts cause companies to hire more and Democrats' skepticism. If companies do hire because of lower tax rates than they would—and if they don't—companies would pay the same tax rate.

> It is time we implement a policy that makes corporate tax cuts contingent on results. We need a result-based corporate tax code.

It's Time Congress Was Introduced to the Concept of ROI

Toward an ROI-Based Corporate Tax Code

It is time we replace our campaign-donation-, lobbyist-driven corporate tax policy with an ROI-based policy driven by financial results. It is time our corporate tax policy is driven

> It is time our corporate tax policy is driven by return on investment, not return on campaign donations and lobbying dollars spent.

by return on investment, not return on campaign donations and lobbying dollars spent.

The concept of ROI is nonexistent when it comes to our corporate tax code. It is absent from the public debate on corporate tax policy. It is also absent in the halls of Congress. I'll never forget discussing the idea of an ROI-based corporate tax policy that bases each company's corporate tax rate on its wage and job growth with a congressional staffer. She looked at me with a forlorn face and replied, "They just don't think that way." Because of this, both policy and debate are missing what really matters: tying company tax rates to each company's level of wages, wage growth, and rate of jobs created by each company in America. What we need to be debating is what wage level jobs need to pay to qualify for a tax break or how many jobs need to be created to qualify for a tax break.

What we need to be debating is what wage level jobs need to pay to qualify for a tax break or how many jobs need to be created to qualify for a tax break.

While Congress doesn't think in terms of ROI, those lobbying Congress do. They lobby Congress to get the most advantageous, highest ROI, no-strings-attached tax cuts for their clients, and the shareholders of USA Inc. pick up the bill. So Congress passes out universal and unconditional tax breaks to all companies like candy, whether they are job creators or destroyers and whether they are raising wages or not. If the purpose of corporate tax cuts is to generate higher wages and more jobs, then at least make receiving the tax cuts contingent on higher wages and more jobs—that's just obvious. Anything else is policy negligence or campaign-donation-influenced malfeasance. It is time our managers, Congress, obtain a better return on tax cut investments. The investment is corporate tax cuts and the returns are better wage growth and more job creation…in the U.S. Why am I repeating this? Because it is such a new concept, it needs to be repeated before it sinks in.

> If the purpose of corporate tax cuts is to generate higher wages and more jobs, then at least make receiving the tax cuts contingent on higher wages and more jobs.

Earned Corporate Tax Cuts

Under the Earned Corporate Tax Cut (ECTC), each company's tax rate would be within its control. Pay higher wages than your industry peers, get a tax cut. Increase wages, get a tax cut. Increase your number of full-time employees in America, get a tax cut. Conversely, if a company pays a lower wage than its peers, doesn't raise wages, and doesn't increase its number of full-time employees in America, its tax rate would remain the same. Companies would have it within their power to lower their tax rate. This approach leads to our first corporate tax solution.

Corporate Tax Solution #1: Base each company's tax rate on its median wage, excluding executives and sales personnel, relative to its industry's median wage level.

Under this solution, companies paying more than their industry peers would see their tax rates reduced, while those paying the same wouldn't see a reduction in taxes.

Corporate Tax Solution #2: Base each company's tax rate on the year-over-year increase in each company's median wage, excluding executives and sales personnel.

These solutions would ensure that the companies paying higher wages and increasing wages receive tax cuts, while those that don't won't. This would finally provide a real incentive for companies to pay higher wages, generating greater wage growth and, as a result, a better return on investment from the corporate tax cuts.

Next, corporate tax rates need to be tied to company job creation...in America.

Corporate Tax Solution #3: Base each company's tax rate on whether it increases its number of American-based full-time employees.

This would finally provide a real incentive for companies to increase hiring in America, generating greater employment growth and, as a result, a better return on investment from the corporate tax cuts.

To ensure that small businesses are on a level playing field with large businesses, we need two additional solutions.

Corporate Tax Solution #4: Base each company's tax rate on the percentage increase in its number of American-based full-time employees.

If a small business owner increases its full-time employees by ten and it only had ten to start with, that is a far more meaningful investment than if a large company with 100,000 employees increases its full-time employee count by ten.

Corporate Tax Solution #5: Base each company's tax rate on the percentage of its total full-time employees that are in the U.S.

This solution would not only benefit small companies, as they would be expected to have a higher percentage of their employees in the U.S., but it would also provide an incentive for larger multinational companies to maintain more of their workforce in the U.S.

Now, some may point out that companies could try and game these solutions by simply making more of their non-U.S.-based employees independent contractors or by outsourcing work done by their global employees to other companies, increasing the percentage of their workforce that is U.S.-based. This leads us to the next corporate tax solution.

Corporate Tax Solution #6: Companies converting full-time employees to independent contractors or outsourcing full-time employees would not be eligible for tax cuts for a period of ten years, and this would be retroactive to 2017, the year the TCJA was passed.

This still leaves the question of taxes paid on overseas profits. The argument has been that these rates need to be lower to encourage companies to bring their foreign-owned profits back to the U.S., based on the hope that the money would be used to hire more Americans. There is a simple solution for this.

Corporate Tax Solution #7: If overseas profits are used to hire more Americans, overseas profits would be taxed at a lower rate. Conversely, if the profits aren't used to hire more Americans, the tax rate would remain the same.

Next, unless companies receive tax cuts *after* they increase employee wages, and/or they increase their number of full-time employees, it will still be a hope-based tax policy. So we need the following solution.

Corporate Tax Solution #8: Corporations qualifying for corporate tax cuts receive the reduced rate *after* they increase wages and/or increase their full-time employees.

Another possible way to game the system is by companies increasing their number of full-time employees at the end of the year to qualify for a tax cut and then fire them at the beginning of the year. There is a solution for this too.

Corporate Tax Solution #9: Only full-time employees that have been employed by the company for a full year count toward a company's full-time employee list, and the end-of-the-year count will be used to determine whether the full-time employee list was increased.

Implementation of solutions 1-9 requires another solution.

Corporate Tax Solution #10: Corporations track and report the increase/decrease in their number of U.S. full-time employees, average wage paid for U.S. full-time employees, whether they converted any full-time employees to independent contractors, and whether they outsourced any full-time employees.

Implementing the Solutions: The ECTC Scorecard

Implementing these solutions requires a "scoring" system that can be used to determine each company's tax rate. Compiling the previously discussed solutions results in the Earned Corporate Tax Cut (ECTC) "scorecard" below. It would be the basis for determining each company's corporate tax rate, a tax rate based on each company's wage levels, wage growth, and job creation in America, all of which are within the control of each company. The scorecard also has the advantage of utilizing a concept—scoring—that Congress and D.C. policymakers are used to.

Earned Corporate Tax Cut Scorecard	
Solutionomics	
Factor	Answer
1. Did the company increase its number of full-time U.S. based employees.[1]	
2. If yes, go to line 3, if no, go to line 4	
3. Pay the standard statutory corporate tax rate	
4. Increase in number full-time employees	
5. Percentage increase in number of full-time employees	
6. Company NAICS Code	
7. Company's average U.S. based full-time employee wage	
8. Percentage of the company's full-time employees based in the U.S.	
9. Earned Corporate Tax	

[1] Employed minimum of 12 months in the U.S.

Source: *Solutionomics*

Some may notice that I am not talking about specific corporate tax rate levels. This is not an oversight. We already have enough debate over tax rate levels, a debate which has had no discussion of connecting tax rate levels to actual wage and job growth. My goal is to introduce and focus on the idea of an ROI-based corporate tax code that ties corporate tax rates to the goal of tax cuts, company's wage levels, wage growth, and job creation.

Benefits of an ROI-Based Corporate Tax Code

Determining each company's tax rate based on its wage levels, wage growth, job growth, and percentage of employees based in the U.S. would have at least ten benefits:

- First, it would create real incentives to increase wages and hiring. As opposed to the TCJA, under the ROI-based ECTC, lower tax rates are contingent on companies increasing hiring and wages—creating a real incentive to pay more and increase hiring.
- Second, if corporate tax cuts were limited to companies increasing hiring and wages, larger tax cuts could be given to those companies, as companies firing Americans would not siphon off tax cuts.
- Third, under the ECTC, companies can control their tax rate, as they are in control of the wages they pay and how many and where they hire employees.
- Fourth, companies paying higher wages than their peers, raising wages, and increasing the number of jobs in America, would finally earn the favorable tax treatment they deserve. For too long, companies paying higher wages, increasing wages, and increasing hiring have in effect been penalized, as companies paying the lowest wages and firing Americans have been freeloading off other companies by receiving the same tax cuts.
- Fifth, the ECTC's targeted tax cuts could generate a better ROI by increasing the wage and employment gains realized per tax-cut dollar, producing a better return on tax cuts.

- Sixth, it could lessen the decline in tax revenues, as only companies creating American jobs would qualify for a lower tax rate.
- Seventh, all of this would be accomplished while increasing the possibility of greater employment and wage growth, as companies would have a real incentive to increase hiring and wages.
- Eighth, it could increase policy certainty by bridging the divide between Republicans pushing for more tax cuts and Democrats pushing for elimination of the TCJA tax cuts. The ECTC would allow Republicans to try and stimulate employment and wage growth through corporate tax cuts while addressing the Democrats' concerns that companies would take the tax cut savings without increase hiring or wages. Instead of continuing to argue over what the economic effects of corporate tax cuts *could* be, corporate tax cuts would be based on the economic effects of *actual* wage and job growth.

> Bridging the gap between both parties is critical given today's increasingly polarized Congress in which wide swings in policy are becoming an increasing risk.

Bridging the gap between both parties is critical, given today's increasingly polarized Congress in which wide swings in policy are becoming an increasing risk. Whether it was passage of the Affordable Care Act, commonly referred to as Obamacare, and Republicans vowing to repeal it or Democrats wanting to repeal or significantly change the TCJA, policy stability is increasingly at risk. This can become a significant hindrance to wage growth and job creation if companies are unsure what tax policies they will be operating under, a very real possibility given calls from one side of the political aisle to lower tax rates further and calls from the other side to eliminate the TCJA's tax cuts.

Ninth, because companies would have an incentive to increase hiring in America and increase the percentage of its workforce based in the U.S., these solutions would eliminate the need to apply punitive tariffs on imported goods. Instead of using tariffs to try and preserve American jobs and encourage job creation in America, corporate tax policy would be used, avoiding further escalating trade tensions. Corporate tax cuts would also be more effective than punitive tariffs targeting an individual country, as these tariffs could be avoided by shifting production to another country, while tax rates tied to American job creation could not be gamed that way.

Corporate tax cuts would also be more effective than punitive tariffs targeting an individual country, as these tariffs could be avoided by shifting production to another country, while tax rates tied to American job creation could not be gamed that way.

Tenth, an ROI-based corporate tax code would finally provide an accurate picture of which companies are generating more American jobs and which are destroying American jobs. It would finally provide insight into which companies are paying higher wages and which companies are not. This would be very different from today's environment in which we are forced to guess.

Potential Objections

Some may argue that solutions 1-10 are too burdensome—just more government paperwork and cost to businesses. First, corporations don't have to do this; it is up to them whether they want to apply for tax cuts. Much like writing off expenses, corporations don't have to report this information, but much like with expenses, if they don't, they won't be able to reduce their tax bill. Second, corporations are already tracking what they pay and who they are hiring and firing. The ECTC would simply have companies report what they are already tracking.

Others might argue that companies may try to game the system, making the ECTC pointless. However, a company trying to game the system does not change the fact that tying corporate tax cuts to company job creation and wages is more efficient than cutting corporate tax cuts unconditionally for all companies in the hope that jobs are created, and wages increase. Additionally, I'd rather have the IRS verifying company job creation and wage growth than have the Treasury Department borrow $1.9 trillion of additional debt in the hope that they get something in return. Last, not implementing an ROI-based corporate tax code because some companies may try to game the system is equivalent to not turning on your car alarm because someone may try and break into your car anyway.

Others may question whether Congress would pass a bill that makes tax cuts contingent on job creation and wages. While they may or may not, think of it this way: If you owned a business and you were told how to increase your return on investment, but your management team wouldn't implement the plan, would you give up on the plan? No! You would change the management.

10. STOP SUBSIDIZING LOW-WAGE STATES POACHING JOBS FROM HIGHER-WAGE STATES

Opportunities to improve our corporate tax policy do not end with federal corporate taxes. There is substantial opportunity for improvement at the state level as well. States currently dole out state corporate tax breaks at a pace that would make even our members of Congress blush. Forty-six states offer corporate tax credits through more than two hundred programs.[44] And they are big spenders. Louisiana reportedly gave away more than $3 billion[45] in corporate tax incentives to attract or retain employers over a five-year period. That is 55 percent[46] of the corporate taxes that would have been collected without the corporate tax credits. But that is a pittance compared to the more than $80 billion[47] of tax breaks offered by states collectively to attract or retain businesses. What if corporations don't deliver the goods? Interestingly, in one case, the town of Ypsilanti in Michigan sued General Motors. However, an

44 Emily Chasan, "Companies Cash In on Tax-Credit Arms Race," *The Wall Street Journal*, June 16, 2014.

45 Marsha Shuler, "Auditor: Tax Credits Cost Louisiana $3 Billion," *The* (Baton Rouge-New Orleans) *Advocate*, March 1, 2014.

46 Ibid.

47 Louise Story, "The United States of Subsidies," *The New York Times*, Dec. 12, 2012

appellate court ruled that assurances of jobs "cannot be evidence of a promise."[48] So get the jobs first!

How can states afford to provide such generous tax breaks? They can't. They rely on the subsidies provided by—you guessed it—our esteemed management known as Congress, all using your taxes. Remember that $3 billion-plus subsidy the state of Louisiana provided corporations? Interestingly, it was estimated that for every $1 of federal taxes Louisiana sent to Washington, Louisiana received $3.35[49] in federal funds. We basically have states using federal money, your taxes, to subsidize their corporate tax breaks, tax breaks they use to steal jobs from other states. It is the equivalent of having the profitable divisions within a company fund the price cuts being offered by the nonprofitable divisions stealing customers away from the profitable divisions. It is crazy. How crazy is it? Consider this: As part of an effort to attract Boeing jobs, South Carolina provided an estimated $900 million in corporate tax incentives, and that doesn't include approximately $33 million in worker training to be provided by the state.[50] And what did the workers gain? A 33 percent pay cut. Wages at the South Carolina Boeing facility are 33 percent or $10 less an hour than wages at the Everett, Washington, facility where the production is being moved from.[51]

---

48 Louise Story, "Corporations Get Tax Deals; States, Cities Pay the Price," *Seattle Times*, Dec. 2, 2012

49 "La. Gets $3.35 in Federal Aid for Every $1 Paid in Federal Taxes, Report Says," *Greater Baton Rouge Business Report*, April 1, 2014.

50 Pamela M. Prah, "Aerospace Manufacturing Takes Off in South," *USA Today*, April 2, 2014.

51 Steve Wilhelm, "Boeing's South Carolina Workers Make $10 Less Per Hour Than Those in Everett," *Puget Sound* (Washington) *Business Journal*, April 8, 2015.

That is also 33 percent less spending power the American consumer will have, and consumer spending makes up nearly 70 percent of gross domestic product. Way to go—we just subsidized a significant reduction in the largest component of GDP.

So how does South Carolina afford that type of incentive? Some may say it can't afford not to offer that size incentive. While that is a pithy response, what made the incentive possible was the following: For every dollar it sent to Washington, South Carolina received $7.87[52] from Washington. Talk about a great return on "investment." What investor wouldn't love to get $7.87 in return for every $1 invested? Small wonder South Carolina could afford to woo Boeing with such a sizable package. But does it make sense to have the federal government subsidizing these types of state corporate tax breaks, especially when it is to replace higher-paying jobs in one state with lower-paying jobs in another state? Think of each state as a separate business division within USA Inc. Would a CEO let its lower-earning divisions use funds from its higher-earning divisions to siphon off business from those very same higher-earning divisions? Of course not. But that is what we are doing. This leads to an obvious solution.

But does it make sense to have the federal government subsidizing these types of state corporate tax breaks, especially when it is to replace higher-paying jobs in one state with lower-paying jobs in another state?

52 Tim Smith, "SC Does Better Than Most in Receiving Federal Dollars," *Greenville* (South Carolina) *News*, Oct. 19, 2014.

Corporate Tax Solution #11: States that are net recipients of federal dollars and offer any type of financial incentive to attract or retain companies immediately repay the difference between what they send to Washington and what they receive from Washington, with interest.

We need higher incomes, not lower incomes.

I'm all for competition, but not federally funded competition, especially when it involves poaching higher-paying jobs and replacing them with lower-paying jobs. We need higher incomes, not lower incomes.

11. MAKING THE INVISIBLE HAND VISIBLE

The Invisible Hand is the concept that consumer actions act like a collective hand that rewards or punishes companies based on company actions. While this can work, it first requires consumers to know what companies are doing, which is not always the case. This leads to our last, but not least, corporate tax policy solution.

Corporate Tax Solution #12: Packaging for products sold in America, regardless of the company nationality, prominently displays what percentage of the total employees (including subcontractors and independent contractors) utilized in the production of the product are American-based.

Having this information would allow consumers to make buying decisions based on which products are the most "American." As we will see in the section on global trade, this will also have the benefit of focusing consumers on American job creation, as opposed to the nationality of a company. In this increasingly interconnected global economy, company nationality is far less important than the jobs companies are creating...in America. As an example, BMW, Nissan, Airbus, and many other foreign companies are creating jobs in America. Conversely, Buick and Cadillac are making cars in China and exporting them to the U.S., while Boeing 737s are rolling off Chinese assembly lines for the first time. I wonder if the laid-off auto workers know they are buying cars which could have been made in the U.S. but instead are made in China. It is time we focus on what each company is contributing to our economy, not a company's nationality.

> It is time we focus on what each company is contributing to our economy, not a company's nationality.

SECTION II

WINNING THE GAME OF GLOBAL TRADE

"Revenge in this case naturally dictates retaliation, and that we should impose the like duties and prohibitions upon importation of some or all or all of their manufactures (goods) into ours."[53]

—Adam Smith, The Wealth of Nations
"I use no beer or cheese in my family, but such as is made in America."[54] *"...[K]eep pace with me in purchasing nothing foreign where an equivalent of domestic...can be obtained...."*[55]

---

53 Adam Smith, *The Wealth of Nations*, Book IV, Chapter II, 489.

54 "George Washington, Madeira, and the Morristown Beer Crisis," *George Washington's Mount Vernon*, https://www.mountvernon.org/the-estate-gardens/food-culture/beer/.

55 Thomas Jefferson to Benjamin Austin, Jan. 9, 1816, in *Founders Online*, National Archives, accessed Jan. 18, 2019

From its founding, America has been faced with a global trading system dominated by countries trying to restrict access to their markets while at the same time clamoring for access to the American market.

While these quotes may sound similar to the rhetoric occurring today, they are quotes from George Washington and Thomas Jefferson. Neither their views nor the circumstances of unequal trade terms which elicited them are new. From its founding, America has been faced with a global trading system dominated by countries trying to restrict access to their markets while at the same time clamoring for access to the American market. Today's trading environment is nothing new.

When it comes to tariffs, sometimes what is new is old. President Donald Trump has been willing to impose tariffs, much to the dismay of his Republican brethren. Dismayed as they may be, Trump is more in line with the first leaders of the Republican Party than they are. Republicans from Abraham Lincoln to Theodore Roosevelt and Herbert Hoover proudly wore the badge of protectionism, associating prosperity with protectionism while claiming Democrats promoting free trade were the agents of English mercantile interests.[56] Early Republicans even castigated free trade, associating it with low wages and the destruction of high wage jobs. Lincoln stated that "…abandonment of the protective policy by the American government must result in an increase of both useless labor, and idleness; and so, in proportion, must produce want and ruin among

56 Alfred Eckes, *Opening America's Market: U.S. Foreign Trade Policy Since 1776* (Chapel Hill, N.C.: The University of North Carolina Press, 1995), 29.

It invites the product of his cheaper labor to this market to destroy the domestic product representing the higher and better paid labor of ours.

our people."[57] Lincoln was arguing that dropping trade protections would harm American labor. In 1892, while giving a speech in Nebraska, future Republican President William McKinley proclaimed in reference to free trade, "It invites the product of his cheaper labor to this market to destroy the domestic product representing the higher and better paid labor of ours."[58]

Today's Republican leaders remain in a state of shock as they watch Trump's willingness to use tariffs in the pursuit of reciprocal trade terms. Perhaps, like Trump, early Republicans focused on what they believed would be the long-term gains in employment and wages over the short-term pain of consumers.

12. THE UNITED STATES OF CHUMPS NO MORE

> *Before we condemn global trade or conversely trumpet its merits as the miracle cure to all our economic problems, we need first to understand the following: The U.S. is nowhere near realizing its potential in global trade.*

---

57 Abraham Lincoln, *Abraham Lincoln: Complete Works, Volume 1,* ed. John G. Nicolay and John Hay (New York: The Century Co., 1894), 95.

58 "An Address by M' Kinley," *The New York Times*, Aug. 3, 1892.

The U.S. is receiving a horrible return on investment when it comes to its global trade policy. In fact, there is a Grand Canyon-like chasm between its potential and today's dismal performance. Just how far short are we falling from the potential? Warren Buffett is reported to have said, "If you are playing poker and you don't know who the chump is, then you likely are the chump." Well, in the world of global trade, that's us. Every country loves to trade with the U.S. because they will likely win.

Before I continue, note that I will address the debate surrounding whether trade deficits matter later in Global Trade Myth #8.

In 2018, twelve of the fifteen largest economies we traded with sold more goods to us than we did to them. That's right, we "lost" 80 percent of the time. Using the analogy of an NFL team, our equivalent record would have been three wins, twelve losses. And it's gotten worse over time. While still embarrassing, in 1993, our record with these same countries was five wins, ten losses.

In 2018, twelve of the fifteen largest economies we traded with sold more goods to us than we did to them. That's right, we "lost" 80 percent of the time.

U.S. Trade in Goods by Country (Millions of U.S. Dollars)	
Country	Deficit/Surplus
China	$ (419,527)
Mexico	$ (80,658)
Germany	$ (68,096)
Japan	$ (67,196)
Italy	$ (31,946)
India	$ (20,847)
Canada	$ (19,056)
S. Korea	$ (17,757)
France	$ (15,815)
Indonesia	$ (12,670)
Russia	$ (14,217)
Spain	$ (4,124)
Brazil	$ 8,457
U.K.	$ 5,530
Australia	$ 15,186

Source: Solutionomics using U.S. Census Bureau Data

Do you think coaches with that type of record last long in the NFL? Yet that is what our country's "coaching staff"—our presidents and Congress—have achieved for us. We're getting beaten so badly in global trade, I wouldn't be surprised if other countries chant, "United States of Chumps, United States of Chumps," at future Olympics.

> I wouldn't be surprised if other countries chant, "United States of Chumps, United States of Chumps," at future Olympics.

Looking specifically at China, after it joined the World Trade Organization in December 2001, the U.S. goods'trading deficit with China increased more than four times in just seventeen years. It now stands at more than $419 billion. The question isn't whether something needs to change in U.S. trade policy; the question is what.

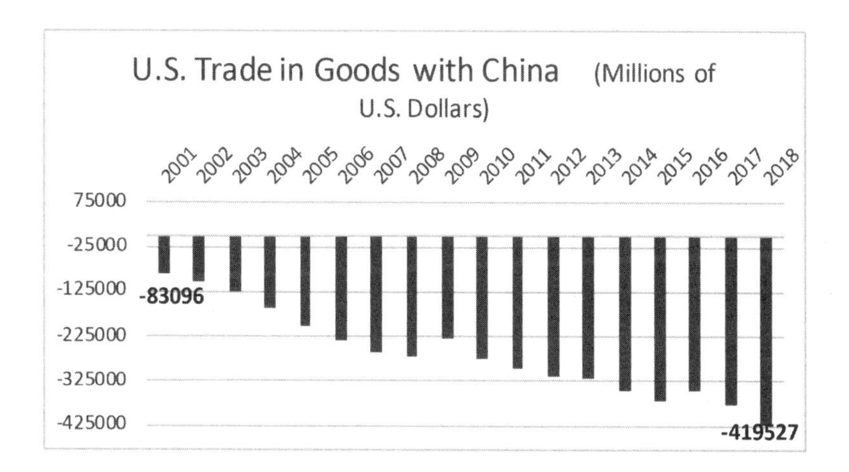

Source: U.S. Census Bureau

While China gets all the media coverage because of its massive $382 billion trade surplus in goods with the United States, according to the Organisation for Economic Cooperation and Development, Germany has the largest trade surplus with the world when looking at goods *and* services. Its surplus is nearly $280 billion, handily beating China's $211 billion. How? Whereas China has a much larger global trade surplus in goods than Germany, China also has a significant global trade deficit in services reducing its goods and services trade surplus with the world, while Germany has a relatively minimal service deficit, allowing it to have the largest surplus in goods and services with the world.

U.S. Trade in Goods by Country (Millions of U.S. Dollars)		
2018	Germany	China
Goods	$ 261,868	$ 395,171
Services	$ (23,138)	$ (233,146)
Net	$ 238,730	$ 162,025

Source: Organisation for Economic Co-operation and Development (OECD)

Germany's global trade surplus is even more impressive when considering that Germany's economy is less than one-third the size of China's. Taking this into account, it is clear that Germany is benefiting far more from global trade in proportion to the size of its economy than China, with Germany's surplus representing 6.4 percent of its GDP vs. China's 0.9 percent of its GDP. In addition to high-quality, advanced, precision products, Germany benefits from a relative currency advantage. The euro makes German products more price-competitive globally than they otherwise would be if Germany went back to using a currency solely reflecting its financial condition. With this advantage, Germany's 2017 imports and exports of goods and services equaled more than 76 percent of its GDP; this compares to 27 percent for the U.S. While President Trump has made it clear he is not happy with the current German trade dynamics, given its elevated dependence on and success in global trade, Germany isn't going to easily give up its advantage in trade.

As impressive as Germany's trading record and ability to benefit from global trade is, Ireland benefits even more in relation to the size of its economy. Ireland's more than $100 billion trade surplus in goods and service, while less than Germany's, was equal to more than 27 percent of its total GDP—a staggering percentage. Ireland owes its global trade prowess to more than luck. Its status as a tax haven for global pharmaceutical companies, along with its significant exports of organic chemicals, drove its impressive trade performance.

Switching back to the global trade losers, not only did the U.S. buy more goods from twelve of the fifteen largest economies it traded with than they bought from the U.S., in 2017, it also set the dubious record of the largest absolute dollar deficit, buying a half-trillion dollars more in goods and services from other countries than they purchased from the U.S. Half a trillion! This would have been much worse given the United States' staggering $751 billion goods deficit if it weren't for its robust $249 billion services surplus. Breaking down the United States'trade deficit into its component parts of goods and services is critical and should not be quickly passed by. It is critical because it highlights the fallacy of the promise that it's okay if we send more goods-producing jobs overseas because we will offset those with services we export to the world. While that would be nice, it certainly hasn't been the reality.

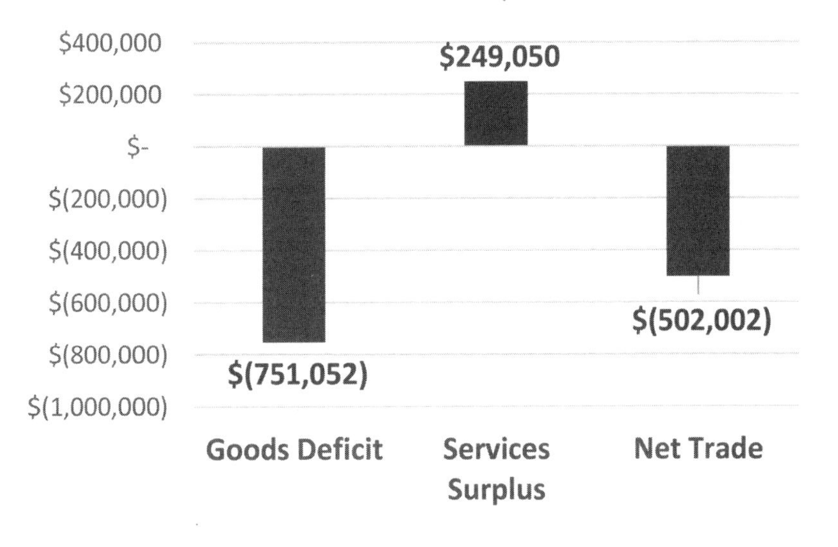

Source: OECD

How do we go from the world's global trading chump to its champ? First, by replacing twelve damaging global trade myths with global trade realities. Second, by understanding that China is consuming far less than its fair share while Germany and Ireland take more from global trade than they contribute. Third, by understanding that global trade agreements are as much about advancing foreign policy goals as they are trade policy.

Before I continue, let me clarify that I am not suggesting global trade is bad. We need to trade with the rest of the world. What I am stating is the fact that, while we are nowhere near realizing our potential, we can do much better—we can move much closer to reaching our global trade potential.

> While we are nowhere near realizing our potential, we can do much better—we can move much closer to reaching our global trade potential.

I am also *not* advocating we suddenly and abruptly pull out of current trade agreements. That would create a significant disruption in global supply chains and global trade. I am, however, asking why the U.S. can't start negotiating more favorable terms that are *phased in over time*? We have the largest, most affluent market in the world. It is the market every multinational company wants and needs to sell to. It is time we start leveraging this to negotiate at least equal trade terms with other countries and, ideally, negotiate more favorable trade terms for the U.S. The President was correct in his speech at the World Economic Forum in January 2018 when he said, "We support free trade, but it needs to be fair and it needs to be reciprocal."

> We have the largest, most affluent market in the world. It is the market every multinational company wants and needs to sell to. It is time we start leveraging this to negotiate at least equal trade terms with other countries.

13. DEBUNKING THE TWELVE MOST DAMAGING GLOBAL TRADE MYTHS

A series of damaging global trade myths is preventing the U.S. from winning the game of global trade. We are basing trade policy on assumptions that are false, leading us to continue losing trade policies. When we, instead, debunk these myths and start basing our trade policy on trade reality, we will have taken the first step toward winning the game of global trade.

One important note: When I refer to or use the names of countries, I am referring to their leaders, not the citizens of the countries referenced.

Global Trade Myth #1: All countries want free and open trade.

There is nothing "free" about trade today. There are all types of barriers to trade. Yet there is a myth that other countries negotiate trade agreements to achieve free trade. Well, if you believe that, I have some oceanfront property in Iowa I'd like to sell you. Other countries use tariffs, quotas, and other trade-restricting policies that benefit them and restrict free trade. They aren't pursuing a system of trade in which consumers choose purely on the merits of each product free of tariffs and quotas. That is a myth that is rarely seen in the real world of global trade. What makes this myth even more damaging is that it is used by those arguing against implementing any form of American trade protections. In their arguments, there is an unspoken assumption that all countries want free and open trade. They infer that the U.S. would somehow be committing a heinous crime if it were to implement any restrictions, when in reality, all countries use protectionism to gain advantage for their products over ours. These arguments and the myth that all countries pursue free trade put the U.S. at a significant disadvantage in the world of global trade. That is the reality, and the U.S. has faced protectionist policies from abroad since its founding.

In reality, all countries use protectionism to gain advantage for their products over ours.

In the 1700s, Britain and France engaged in what is called mercantilism. Mercantilism is a policy in which protectionist trade measures are used by a country to try and export more than it imports. Britain and France restricted access to their markets placing U.S. goods at a competitive disadvantage. How significant of a problem was this? The first American tariff was passed in 1789 and signed by President Washington. Its preamble stated that its purpose was for "the encouragement and protection of manufactures."[59]

America still faces protectionist measures abroad. President Trump noted this reality during his 2018 World Economic Forum speech in Davos, Switzerland, when he said, "We expect the leaders of other countries to protect their interests." Contrary to the idealistic theory of a world in which all countries place creating a

59 Alfred Eckes, *Opening America's Market*, 14.

> The reality is that every country is protectionist—every country tries to tilt the playing field in its favor through disproportionate tariffs, quotas, and other means.

global system of free trade above their personal interests, the reality is that every country is protectionist—every country tries to tilt the playing field in its favor through disproportionate tariffs, quotas, and other means.

The Founding Fathers understood this reality and even those who preferred free trade, such as Thomas Jefferson, supported trade sanctions in the face of continued unfair trade practices, understanding that free trade remained more of a theory than a reality.[60] Yet today, despite the obvious efforts of other countries to gain an unfair trade advantage through blatantly protectionist policies, some object to implementing trade policies which would merely place America on equal footing with other countries, labeling these efforts as protectionist—as if no other country is protectionist! This wouldn't be protectionist; it would be leveling the playing field. It would be pursuing the same policy of trade reciprocity pursued by our Founding Fathers in response to the protectionist policies they faced globally.

> It would be pursuing the same policy of trade reciprocity pursued by our Founding Fathers in response to the protectionist policies they faced globally.

If every other country is trying to get the best trade terms and engaging in protectionism, whether it is through

60 Ibid., 13.

disproportionately high tariffs, quotas, or other means, why should we play by a different set of rules? Why should we carry the banner of free and open trade while other countries trade us into bankruptcy through their protectionist policies?

> Why should we carry the banner of free and open trade while other countries trade us into bankruptcy through their protectionist policies?

None other than the ultimate proponent of free trade, Adam Smith, in the face of tariffs advocated for retaliatory measures, stated, "Revenge in this case naturally dictates retaliation, and that we should impose the like duties and prohibitions upon the importation of some or all of the manufactures into ours." Smith even went on to endorse duties and prohibitions as good policy when confronted with the like, stating, "There may be good policy in retaliation of this kind, when there is a probability that they will procure the repeal of the high duties or prohibitions complained of."[61] To do otherwise is not only naïve, it is a dereliction of duty by our elected officials.

> *"There may be good policy in retaliation of this kind, when there is a probability that they will procure the repeal of the high duties or prohibitions."*
>
> *—Adam Smith*

Global Trade Reality #1: All countries pursue a trade advantage. All countries are protectionist.

61 Adam Smith, *The Wealth of Nations*, Book IV, Chapter II, 490.

Can the U.S. negotiate better terms? Of course. As we noted previously, we have the most desirable market in the world. It is the market every multinational company wants—no, needs—to sell to. It is time we start leveraging this to negotiate more favorable trade terms with other countries.

Trade Solution #1: *At a minimum, negotiate equal trade terms and, ideally, negotiate more favorable terms for the U.S.*

Global Trade Myth #2: Tariffs and quotas are always bad.

While tariffs and quotas are not the first choice, there is a myth that tariffs and quotas are *always* bad. Like most things in life, this absolute is false. It is just as false as the other extreme that tariffs on all products all the time are always effective. Some tariffs and quotas can be effective and even necessary in a world in which, as we just saw, all countries are protectionist. Often tariffs are merely self-defenses, a reciprocal response to the protectionist measures the U.S. faces every day. These are very different from punitive tariffs, which involve levying tariffs well in excess of the tariffs placed on American goods by other countries. U.S. presidents and members of Congress take an oath to protect the U.S. against foreign threats. It is time they begin fulfilling that obligation in relation to the threats faced from the aggressive protectionist policies pursued by foreign countries.

Often tariffs are merely self-defenses, a reciprocal response to the protectionist measures the U.S. faces every day.

> Note: Tariffs and quotas are not the first choice. Sometimes, however, select strategic tariffs and quotas, not universal or punitive tariffs and quotas, can work and are necessary. When used, it is important that they are gradually implemented to allow companies to reconfigure supply chains, avoiding suddenly disrupting supply chains. The purpose of strategic tariffs is to, at a minimum, level the playing field; that is, achieve trade provision reciprocity and ideally gain an advantage for the U.S., just as other countries are and have been successful in gaining an advantage.

Reagan and China Prove Tariffs and Quotas Can Work

Up until July 2018, China placed a 25 percent tariff on imported cars while the U.S. had a 2.5 percent tariff on cars.[62] How did each country fare with these disparate tariffs? Opponents of tariffs would have predicted damage to China's automobile industry and gains for the U.S. What really happened? China is now the number one producer of cars. China produced nearly 25 million passenger vehicles in 2017, a 4,000 percent increase from its 2000 levels of 605,000, not coincidentally the year before it joined the World Trade Organization (WTO). In just seventeen years, China went from producing less than 15 percent of the world's passenger vehicles to more than one-third of the world's vehicles. How did the U.S. fare during the same time frame? It's not pretty. U.S. car production declined from 5.5 million in 2000 to barely 3 million

62 Trefor Moss, "China to Cut Import Tariff on Autos to 15% from 25%," *The Wall Street Journal*, May 22, 2018.

> During the time when China had 25 percent tariffs and the U.S. had 2.5 percent tariffs, U.S. car production *declined* 45 percent while China's production *increased* more than 4,000 percent.

in 2017—a 45 percent decline.[63] During the time when China had 25 percent tariffs and the U.S. had 2.5 percent tariffs, U.S. production *declined* 45 percent while China's production *increased* more than 4,000 percent. Still think tariffs don't work? In 1965, the U.S. implemented a 25 percent tariff on light trucks. What happened? From 1965 to 2015, commercial vehicle production in the U.S. increased more than 450 percent while passenger car production declined by half.

More recently, in response to a U.S. International Trade Commission recommendation, President Trump placed up to a 50 percent tariff on washing machines. Again, opponents of tariffs would predict the end of clean clothes at a reasonable price. However, companies impacted by the tariffs, LG and Samsung, are building production facilities in the U.S.[64] While some have argued that the decision to build production facilities in the U.S. was unrelated to the tariffs, it is a reasonable assumption that, at a minimum, production levels in the U.S. will be greater than initially anticipated in response to tariffs as they seek to produce more tariff-exempt washing machines.

---

63 International Organization of Motor Vehicle Manufacturers.

64 "How Asian Giants Can Counter Trump's Washing Machine Tariffs," Bloomberg, *The Straits* (Singapore) *Times*, Jan. 23, 2018, https://www.straitstimes.com/world/united-states/how-asian-giants-can-counter-trumps-washing-machine-tariffs.

In response to another recent U.S. International Trade Commission recommendation, Trump placed tariffs on solar panel imports. Why was this necessary? Nine of the world's ten largest solar panel manufacturers are non-American, even though the U.S. pioneered the technology. Notably, seven of the top ten solar panel manufacturers are Chinese companies.[65] Why the U.S. decline? The U.S. had been the leader in solar panel technology for three decades. Then Chinese competitors entered the market, offering significant price discounts fulfilling the Chinese government's need to find more jobs for their massive population. This crushed U.S. solar panel manufacturers, which were setting solar panel prices based on profits.[66] Done selectively, tariffs can combat this "jobs over profits" mentality that we will see in Global Trade Myth #3 dominates the Chinese state-owned enterprises. Some argue this is a mistake and that we should always purchase from other countries the goods they can produce for less than we can. We will see later in Global Trade Myth #11 that this argument overlooks a key assumption that is not true today - having enough high paying jobs for those displaced

> The fact is that more and more middle-skilled jobs are leaving America or being automated, leaving lower-paying jobs for the displaced workers. We can do better.

65 "The Top Solar Panel Manufacturers in the United States," EnergySage, https://news.energysage.com/best-solar-panel-manufacturers-usa/.

66 John Fialka, "Why China Is Dominating the Solar Industry," *Scientific American*, Dec. 19, 2016, https://www.scientificamerican.com/article/why-china-is-dominating-the-solar-industry/.

when jobs are overseas. The fact is that more and more middle-skilled jobs are leaving America or being automated, leaving lower-paying jobs for the displaced workers. We can do better.

> Even just the threat of tariffs and increasingly pro-American trade rhetoric can impact major manufacturing location decisions.

How effective can tariffs be? Even just the threat of tariffs and increasingly pro-American trade rhetoric can impact major manufacturing location decisions. The multinational electronics manufacturing company Foxconn counted the escalating trade dispute with the U.S. as one of the reasons it decided to build a massive new $10 billion LCD manufacturing facility that comes with the possibility of 13,000 jobs in Wisconsin. A special adviser to Foxconn, Louis Woo, was quoted in the *Financial Times* as saying, "That's one of the reasons why we are here, because of the escalation of the trade dispute between the two biggest trading partners."[67] Or consider Toyota's one-third increase in its U.S. investments by 2021. Toyota's chief executive of North American operations said, "I'd be disingenuous if I said we didn't have our eye on trade" while also indicating that President Trump's policies on trade impacted their plans to shift more activity to the U.S.[68]

Tariffs aren't the only trade tool that has been proven effective. In 1981, President Reagan instituted quotas on Japanese auto

---

67 Patti Waldmeir, "Foxconn Tells the Story Trump Wants U.S.to Hear," *Financial Times*, June 27, 2018.

68 Adrienne Roberts, "Toyota Steps Up U.S. Investment," *Wall Street Journal*, March 15, 2019.

imports. Thirty-five years later, in 2016, Toyota, Honda, and Nissan produce more than three million vehicles in the U.S.,[69] while some American automakers produce less than half of the vehicles they sell in the U.S. in American factories.[70]

In 2016, Toyota, Honda, and Nissan produce more than three million vehicles in the U.S., while some American automakers produce less than half of the vehicles they sell in the U.S. in American factories.

% of Vehicles Sold in the U.S. Also Made in the U.S.	
Acura	***71%***
Toyota	***61%***
Nissan	**55%**

Source: Time.com

GM to Taxpayers Who Bailed Them Out—"We're Outta Here!"

GM received a $49.5 billion taxpayer-funded bailout during the financial crisis, a bailout in which the U.S. taxpayer lost $11.2

69 "Reality Check: Was Trump Right About Japanese Cars Sold in the U.S.?" BBC.com, Nov. 11, 2017.

70 David Johnson, "See Which Car Companies Are the Most American," *Time*, March 2, 2017.

billion.[71] General Motors subsequently made more than $38 billion,[72] GM is now warning that it will move more production overseas—not exactly an attitude of gratitude for everything the U.S. taxpayer did to save GM. But this would be nothing new.

GM already produces a number of its vehicles outside of the U.S., ships them to the U.S., and sells them to U.S. taxpayers. That's right, GM imports cars they make abroad and then sells them to U.S. consumers. These include the Cadillac XTS, Cadillac CT6 plug-in version, and Buick Regal, among others. GM isn't the only "American" automotive manufacturer making vehicles it sells in the U.S. outside of the U.S. Lincoln assembles a mere 17 percent of its vehicles sold in the U.S. within the U.S., while Chrysler assembles a still meager 33 percent of the vehicles it sells in the U.S. within the U.S.[73] With Acura, Toyota, and Nissan each making more than 50 percent of the cars they sell in the U.S. at U.S. factories, which automakers really are the most "American?" Which are the most patriotic?

> It is time U.S. consumers look beyond the car company's nationality to where vehicles are being assembled.

What can the American taxpayer do—look for vehicles assembled in the U.S., which, oddly enough, would often mean buying more foreign brands? In

71 Sam Frizell, "General Motors Bailout Cost American Taxpayers $11.2 Billion," *Time*, April 30, 2014.

72 *Solutionomics* calculations, using Chris Isidore, "GM Made $22.6 Billion. We Lost $10.6 Billion," CNNMoney, May 29, 2014, and subsequent years' profits as reported by Yahoo Finance

73 Johnson, "See Which Car Companies."

this increasingly connected world of global production, it is time U.S. consumers look beyond the car company's nationality to where vehicles are being assembled.

Congress and the President also have a key role to play. As we saw previously, under the TCJA, companies like GM can move production overseas, reduce their American workforce, increase their foreign workforce, and benefit from the same recently passed tax cuts as companies increasing production in the U.S. and hiring more Americans. Talk about a bad ROI for the American taxpayer.

As we also saw previously in the section on corporate taxes, there is a way to incentivize more U.S. production. Under the previously outlined corporate tax solutions #3 and #5, companies increasing the number of American-based full-time employees and the percentage of their total full-time employees that are in the U.S.would pay lower tax rates. These solutions would directly address GM's threats of moving more production overseas. If GM reduced its American workforce, its tax rate would return to the level it was before the TCJA was passed. GM is free to operate as it sees best for its shareholders, and the U.S.is free to operate its tax policy that generates the best ROI for the American taxpayer. Last, given that taxpayers lost $11.2 billion in the bailout of GM, shouldn't taxpayers be receiving discounts on GM cars as opposed to threats of moving more production overseas? Instead, GM is sending a very unpatriotic message.

> Given that taxpayers lost $11.2 billion in the bailout of GM, shouldn't taxpayers be receiving discounts on GM cars as opposed to threats of moving more production overseas?

Making Competition from Low-Wage Countries Even Worse

Where goods are produced not only impacts the number and quality of jobs available in America—it impacts wages. What happened to automobile industry wages in the U.S.as production decreased in the U.S.and American automakers moved production to China? They declined. GM and Chrysler implemented a two-tier pay system. Long-serving employees would be paid $29 an hour while new employees would be paid $16 an hour.[74] Why did the United Auto Workers accept such a steep cut to new employee wages? "Free trade" and competition from much lower global wages. In 2014, Audi, BMW, and Nissan had union contracts in place that paid workers in Mexico a minimum of $1 an hour and a maximum of $4 an hour.[75] If approximately 70 percent of U.S.GDP is determined by consumption, do we really want American wages declining and moving closer toward wages in Mexico and other depressed-wage countries, placing even more downward pressure on consumers' wages?

If approximately 70 percent of U.S.GDP is determined by consumption, do we really want American wages declining?

Another common justification for blindly and unconditionally accepting the pressure imported products place on American wages is that the lower prices of the imported goods benefit consumers. First, as we will see in myth #9, not all the cost savings associated

74 Michael Collins, "The Threat of Declining Wages," *IndustryWeek*, Nov. 29, 2016.

75 Mark Stevenson, "In Mexico, $2 Per Hour Workers Make $40,000 SUVs," Associated Press, Sept. 25, 2017.

with closing U.S. plants, firing American workers, moving production overseas, and then selling the goods back to the U.S. are passed on to the American consumer. Second, as we will see in myth #10, imported products aren't cheap to those who have lost their jobs and/or had to take lower-paying jobs with no health insurance. Third, while toys and electronics may be cheaper, the cost of big-ticket items that eat up most of a family's budget including housing, education, and health care are rising rapidly.

Imported products aren't cheap to those who have lost their jobs and/or had to take lower-paying jobs with no health insurance.

Why would we knowingly enter a race to the wage bottom? Why would we reduce not only the number of better-paying jobs, but the wages of the remaining jobs? Why are we following trade policy that places downward pressure on pay for the very consumers that 70 percent of our economic growth is dependent on?

Why are we following trade policy that places downward pressure on pay for the very consumers that 70 percent of our economic growth is dependent on?

It isn't just the major automobile manufacturers setting up shop outside of the U.S. Automobile parts suppliers have shifted significant production outside of the U.S.as well. In 2006, the automobile parts supplier Delphi sold or closed twenty-one of its twenty-nine plants in the U.S., eliminating twenty thousand jobs or two-thirds of its workforce while shifting operations overseas to China and Mexico, whereas, in 2017, it employed approximately seventy

That is the impact of naïve trade policies based on idealistic myths concocted outside the real world.

thousand workers. Why? Lower wages. The CEO in 2006, Robert Miller, said U.S. workers were overpaid, so he sought lower wages abroad and he found them. Jobs that used to pay $30 an hour are now being performed by people making $1 an hour. Not only were jobs lost but wages at the remaining Delphi operations in Warren, Ohio, were cut nearly in half, from $29 an hour to $16.50.[76] That is the impact of naïve trade policies based on idealistic myths concocted outside the real world.

Now, if you are reading this and thinking, "They should be grateful for $16.50 an hour, as opposed to making minimum wage," don't forget: 70 percent of GDP is driven by consumer spending. The more consumers make, the more they can consume, increasing GDP. Don't begrudge your fellow American's higher wages. Hope for higher wages, as that person making the higher wage just became a customer for the products the company you work for is producing!

Don't begrudge your fellow American's higher wages. Hope for higher wages, as that person making the higher wage just became a customer for the products the company you work for is producing!

Lower wages also increase dependence on welfare programs, increasing U.S. and state deficits. In 2016, more than a third of

76 Kate Linthicum, "A Tale of Two Cities: What Happened When Factory Jobs Moved From Warren, Ohio to Juarez, Mexico," *Los Angeles Times*, Feb. 17, 2017.

manufacturing production workers employed in nonsupervisory positions used at least one government-provided assistance program.[77] Higher wages can reduce the U.S. deficit by decreasing utilization rates of and spending on welfare programs. It is better to have companies paying employees to make things than the government paying welfare.

It is better to have companies paying employees to make things than the government paying welfare.

Selective tariffs and other trade tools implemented *gradually* to allow manufacturers to reconfigure supply chains can be part of an effective trade policy. The idea that tariffs and other trade tools are always losers is not supported by the facts. Just ask Chinese government officials if they think they are losing or winning in the production of cars.

While there is a common and loud argument that tariffs should never be used because they are protectionist, this is at best a misinformed argument and at worst disingenuous. Either way, it contributes to the elimination of better-paying jobs, places downward pressure on wages, and rising trade deficits. Arguing against tariffs based on claims of protectionism is naïve when every other

It is time we stop using claims of protectionism to disqualify any changes to current trade policy when the reality is that all countries are protectionist.

77 Kate Gibson, "What Factory and Fast-Food Workers Have in Common," CBS News, May 17, 2016.

country in the world is protectionist and using tariffs to gain a trade advantage. It is time we stop using claims of protectionism to disqualify any changes to current trade policy when the reality is that all countries are protectionist.

Global Trade Reality #2: Tariffs and quotas can be effective.

Trade Solution #2: Selectively and gradually leverage tariffs and quotas to first level the global playing field and then tilt it to America's advantage.

Rather than continuing to meekly accept higher tariffs and quotas on our goods while we let other countries flood the U.S. market with their goods, gradually begin implementing tariffs and quotas equal to those that other countries place on our goods. Second, leverage the highly affluent and desirable U.S. market to negotiate terms that give the U.S.an advantage in trade.

Global Trade Myth #3: All countries and their companies are driven by the profit motive.

Imagine you run a business and one of your competitors has many family members it needs to support. These include cousins, brothers, uncles, aunts, and other family members. Rather than giving handouts to all of them, your competitor employs them in the family business. It doesn't really need all of them, but it employs them anyway. Since your competitor is paying them, it might as well be producing something, so the company produces more and more. As a result, your competitor floods the market with goods that were produced based on providing jobs for family members rather than profits, so the goods are priced to generate demand rather than profit. That is what the U.S.is faced with: State-owned enterprises (SOEs) pricing goods to generate work for its citizens as opposed to profits, making it difficult for American companies to compete.

The return SOEs are seeking on their investments is jobs, not profits.

The U.S.is faced with state-owned enterprises pricing goods to generate work for its citizens as opposed to profits, making it difficult for American companies to compete.

China's Key Advantage: No Need to Make a Profit

It is estimated that Chinese SOEs account for 25 percent to 30 percent of the country's industrial production. This percentage is as high as 90 percent in certain sectors. They also account for 17 percent of urban employment and 22 percent of industrial profits.[78] China has more than 100,000 SOEs and, during the first ten months of 2015, SOEs earned $6 trillion,[79] a substantial sum by any measure. Some of these SOEs are very large, with forty-seven of the 106 owned by the central government qualifying for the global *Fortune 500* list.[80] SOEs dominate manufacturing and Chinese equity markets. Forty percent of China's manufacturing is

78 "State-Owned Enterprises, Overcapacity, and China's Market Economy Status," "2016 Annual Report to Congress," U.S.-China Economic and Security Review Commission, Chapter 1, Section 2.

79 Sean Miner, "Commitments on State-Owned Enterprises," in Trans-Pacific Partnership: An Assessment, ed. Cathleen Cimino-Isaacs and Jeffrey Schott (Washington, D.C.: Peterson Institute for International Economics, 2016).

80 Wendy Leutert, "Challenges Ahead in China's Reform of State-Owned Enterprises," *Asia Policy*, no. 21 (January 2016).

state-owned, while 70 percent of the value of Chinese-listed companies is attributed to state-owned enterprises.[81]

> Forty percent of China's manufacturing is state-owned, while 70 percent of the value of Chinese-listed companies is attributed to state-owned enterprises

These entities are not in business for high profit margins. By one calculation, the average annual rate of return of SOEs when state subsidies are removed is dismal—6.29 percent.[82] Yet they keep operating and flooding global markets with noneconomic goods. Why? Jobs. It is estimated that China needs to produce one million new jobs every month[83] versus less than 75,000 in America.[84] That is why the return on investment they prize is job creation. China's SOEs are more akin to nonprofit jobs programs providing jobs, not profits, than for-profit entities. They are a cornerstone of China's brilliant global trade strategy: China pays its people to produce goods, providing jobs for its citizens while driving U.S. industries into the ground, leaving us to pay people

---

81 Eric Ng, "China Must Shrink State-Owned Enterprises if It Wants Reforms to Succeed, Says Former WTO Chief," *South China Morning Post*, April 11, 2018.

82 Agatha Kratz, "Reforming China's State-Owned Enterprises," *China Perspectives*, March 15, 2013.

83 Saheli Roy Choudhury, "Reporter's Notebook: China's Shedding Its Copycat Image With Innovation After Innovation," CNBC, July 18, 2017.

84 Greg Robb, "U.S. Can Add as Few as 50,000 Jobs Per Month and Still Be Healthy, Fed Study Finds," *MarketWatch*, Oct. 24, 2016.

that aren't producing things: China produces goods, USA Inc. produces welfare checks.

China pays its people to produce goods, providing jobs for its citizens while driving U.S. industries into the ground, leaving us to pay welfare to our citizens.

China Produces Things, We Write Welfare Checks

In the U.S., the approach is different. For the "family" members that we cannot profitably employ in our businesses, we write welfare checks. So we write welfare checks while non-capitalist countries use state-owned enterprises as jobs programs. As you can imagine, it is very difficult for American companies that must achieve certain ROI targets to compete with these state-owned enterprises. It can become impossible, and when it does, plants are moved overseas or the businesses are closed altogether. Then everyone looks around and says in disbelief, "Gee, why are all the jobs going overseas?" This isn't rocket science: When competing countries view their SOEs as welfare programs providing jobs without regard for profit, and your trade policy doesn't take this into account, of course you are going to lose out in the world of global trade. Even worse, we borrow the money from China to buy the goods from the Chinese enterprises that are putting U.S. industries out of business.

We borrow the money from China to buy the goods from the Chinese enterprises that are putting U.S. industries out of business.

Global Trade Reality #3: Countries with state-owned enterprises make production decisions based on increasing employment levels, not profit levels: They produce goods, we produce welfare checks.

Global Trade Myth #4: Foreign countries will buy more American goods.

There is a myth that the increasing number of middle-class consumers in foreign countries will automatically choose American products over their home country's products. Why will they automatically buy American goods? Are they any less nationalistic than we are? Do they not care about their own country? Nationalism is alive and well everywhere. We saw an example of this when the United Kingdom voted to leave the European Union. Nationalism is prevalent among countries with all forms of government ranging from democratic to autocratic. Countries with non-democratic forms of government are especially inclined to use nationalism to promote and maintain loyalty to the government. These countries have an even greater incentive to use trade to provide jobs for their people to avoid civil unrest and their leaders being forcibly removed from power. Even if the rising global middle class wanted to choose American goods, they will be constrained. As an example, through protectionism, Chinese leaders limit American products being sold at the expense of Chinese products. As we saw previously, until recently, foreign automakers faced a 25 percent tariff on vehicles not assembled in China, while if they assemble cars in China, they must enter into 50/50 joint ventures with local partners. China announced a plan in 2014 to produce 50 percent of the computer chips it consumes by 2020.[85] The massive trade imbalance

85 Clay Chandler, "Why China Is Emerging as a Tech Superpower to Rival the U.S.," *Fortune*, Nov. 21, 2017.

between China and the U.S. is not an accident. It is the result of many factors including the Chinese government's nationalistic trade policies and a long line of U.S. Presidents and members of Congress failing the American people.

> The massive trade imbalance between China and the U.S. is not an accident, it is the result of the Chinese government's nationalistic trade policies and a long line of U.S. Presidents and members of Congress failing the American people.

And the trade effects are undeniable. From the first full year when China entered the World Trade Organization in 2002 to 2018, the U.S. increased its purchase of Chinese goods by nearly $370 billion while China only increased its purchase of U.S. goods by $89 billion.[86] There is no reason to think this imbalance is going to dramatically change in the near future, because there is no reason to think China is going to voluntarily change its nationalistic trade policies when it has so many people to employ.

China Not Consuming Its Fair Share

China's population is four times greater than the United States' population. However, in 2018, China exported more than four times[87] as many goods to the U.S. as the U.S. exported to China. So much for China's rising middle class buying a disproportionate

86 U.S.Census Bureau.

87 Ibid.

China exported more than four times as many goods to the U.S. as the U.S. exported to China.

share of American goods. Based on the most recent trade imbalance, apparently the American consumer is still king, buying more and more Chinese products. Why is this?

U.S. Trade in Goods by Country (Millions of U.S. Dollars)		
2018	China to U.S.	U.S. to China
Exports	$ 539,676	$ 120,148

Source: U.S. Census Bureau

In addition to the nationalism previously mentioned, there are other causes contributing to this outsized disparity in the China-U.S. trade in goods, including:

- China's immense levels of production and need to offload the excess to the rest of the world by any means
- Average tariffs nearly three times that of the U.S. (10 percent versus 3.4 percent for the U.S.)[88]

88 World Trade Organization, Organisation for Economic Co-operation and Development (OECD).

- Requirements for U.S. companies to produce in China in return for market access
- A myriad of additional trade measures meant to increase sales of Chinese goods and limit U.S. companies' sales

What is often overlooked is that the Chinese consumer is not consuming his fair share. Not only is China flooding global markets with noneconomic exports while limiting access to its market, it is consuming far less, on average, than most other countries. While there is much talk of China's expanding middle class, Chinese consumers make much less than American consumers, and importantly, save far more of what they make than American consumers. Not only is China flooding global markets with noneconomic exports while limiting access to its market, it is consuming far less, on average, than most other countries.

Not only is China flooding global markets with noneconomic exports while limiting access to its market, it is consuming far less, on average, than most other countries.

According to the Organisation for Economic Co-operation and Development (OECD), while U.S. consumers spend the equivalent of $0.97 of every dollar of GDP, Chinese consumers only spent $0.53.[89] Put another way, U.S. consumers saved around 3-4 percent on average, while China's consumers saved 47 percent. For a broader perspective, the average country tracked by the OECD spent more than $0.92 of every GDP dollar,[90] much more than the

89 OECD.

90 Ibid.

$0.53 spent by China's consumers. Clearly, China's disproportionately low consumption rate makes it difficult for the U.S.to have an equal trade balance in goods, especially having dispelled the myth that China will magically choose to buy more American goods.

Exacerbating this imbalance in saving is the much lower income earned by Chinese workers. While the average U.S. manufacturing employee earned more than $39.01 per hour in 2016, the average urban manufacturing employee in China is estimated to have earned $4.26 per hour.[91]

Assuming $4.26 per hour and accounting for purchasing power parity, on average, each U.S. manufacturing job sent to China results in a more than $60,000 reduction in purchasing power, a 77 percent decline.

TRADE IN GOODS AND SERVICES
(MILLIONS OF U.S. DOLLARS)

2017	Germany	China
Goods	$303,076	$476,146
Services	$-23,532	$-265,417
Net	$279,545	$210,728

Source: Solutionomics using Congressional Research Service data

91 Marc Levinson, "U.S. Manufacturing in International Perspective," Congressional Research Service, Feb. 21, 2018, https://fas.org/sgp/crs/misc/R42135.pdf.

China's aggressive noneconomic production activities, conservative spending, and lower wages are a problem not just for the U.S., but the world, resulting in a significant imbalance in its goods exports and imports. In 2017, China exported 27.4 percent[92] more in value than it imported. China was a net taker from global consumption in relation to how much it sells to the world.

China	Millions of U.S. Dollars
Exports	$2,216,458
Imports	$1,740,312
Exports vs. Imports	+27.4%

Source: OECD

Conversely, the U.S. imported 34 percent[93] more than it exported. The U.S. was a net-positive contributor to global consumption in relation to how much it sells the world.

92 OECD.
93 Ibid.

U.S.	Millions of U.S. Dollars
Exports	***$1,550,720***
Imports	***$2,361,932***
Exports vs. Imports	***-34.3%***

Source: OECD

While quotas, tariffs, forced technology transfers, and mandating U.S. companies partner with Chinese companies contribute to the U.S. goods deficit with China and have gotten all the headlines, conservative spending on the part of China's consumers is a critical element that is often overlooked.

As we can now see, access to China's market is only one part of the problem. China's limited willingness to contribute to global demand at rates equal to the rest of the world must also be addressed. So much for the myth that it's okay if we send more jobs overseas because Chinese consumers will buy more American products.

Global Trade Reality #4: Leaders of all countries want to sell more of their country's products.

Global Trade Myth #5: "American" means American-made.

Even if other countries did buy more goods produced by American companies, it wouldn't be as much of a benefit as some would assume. Why? Many "American" products, including some of the most iconic American products, sold overseas are also made overseas, not by American workers. Remember the classic red Radio Flyer red wagon? In 2004, production was moved from Chicago to China. The Chinese may be buying the little red wagons, but Americans aren't making them anymore. Surely Barbie, the All-American girl, is all-American-made? Nope. Barbie doll maker Mattel produces it overseas. If Chinese children are playing with the American icon Barbie, she may have been made by Chinese children. Ironic, isn't it? Or what about those trendy Converse Chuck Taylors and some Nike-owned products? Not made in America. All those Levi's being worn around the world? The odds are pretty good they are made by someone other than an American worker.[94] President Trump highlighted the difference between American-owned and American-made, citing the beloved Oreo, which is American-owned but now partially produced in Mexico.[95] He thought it was such a problem that he would do his part, claiming he would never eat another Oreo—now that's a high level of personal commitment

Many "American" products, including some of the most iconic American products, sold overseas are also made overseas, not by American workers.

94 Mike Stewart, "5 American Icons Made in China," *ITI Manufacturing*, July 31, 2014, https://www.itimanufacturing.com/news/5-american-icons-made-china/.

95 Chuck Berman, "End of an Era: Chicago's Last Oreo Line Shut Down Friday," *Chicago Tribune*, July 8, 2016.

to improving our trade performance. Whether it is Levi's, Nikes, Oreos, or the iconic Barbie doll, they aren't made in America.

But it doesn't stop there. Not only are "American" goods made overseas by foreign workers to sell to the local population, "American" companies are making goods overseas and then exporting them to the U.S. The Buick Encore is an "American" SUV sold in America but made in South Korea, where Buick has manufactured low-cost vehicles for more than a decade.[96] It's not just Buick building "American" cars outside of the U.S. for sale to U.S. consumers; American consumers are able to purchase a Cadillac CT6 plug-in made in China complete with a South Korean-supplied battery pack.[97] So much for the assumption that sending jobs overseas is okay because the newly employed overseas workers will buy American made goods.

"American" is meaning less and less. While American brands Buick and Cadillac make cars overseas by employing foreign workers and export them to the U.S. for sale, multiple foreign automobile companies are making cars in the U.S. Below are "American" cars made outside of the U.S. and "foreign" cars made in the U.S., leaving us to ask: Which brand is truly "American"?

While American brands Buick and Cadillac make cars overseas by employing foreign workers and export them to the U.S. for sale, multiple foreign automobile companies are making cars in the U.S.

96 Norihiko Shirouzu and Hyunjoo Jin, "GM Plans Gradual Pullout of South Korea as Labor Costs Surge," Reuters, Aug. 11, 2013.

97 Danny King, "Chinese-Made Cadillac CT6 Plug-In Starts U.S. Sales," *Autoblog*, April 13, 2017.

Manufacturer	Model	Location
Cadillac	XTS	Canada
Chevrolet	Equinox	Canada
Dodge	Challenger/Charger	Canada
Ford	Edge	Canda
Buick	Envision	China
Cadillac	CT6	China
Ford	Focus	China
Buick	Regal	Germany/Canada
Jeep	Renegade	Italy
Chevrolet	Silverado (4 door)	Mexico
Chevrolet	Cruze (hatchback)	Mexico
Chevrolet	Trax	Mexico
Honda	Pilot	**USA - AL**
Honda	Odyssey	**USA - AL**
Honda	Ridgeline	**USA - AL**
Hyundai	Sonata	**USA - AL**
Mercedes-Benz	R Class	**USA - AL**
Mercedes-Benz	GL	**USA - AL**
Mercedes-Benz	M/GLE	**USA - AL**
Hyundai	SantaFe	**USA - GA**
Kia	Optima	**USA - GA**
Kia	Sorento	**USA - GA**
Honda	Civic	**USA - IN**
Subaru	Legacy	**USA - IN**
Subaru	Outback	**USA - IN**
Toyota	Highlander	**USA - IN**
Toyota	Camry	**USA - IN, KY**
Toyota	Tundra	**USA - IN, TX**
Toyota	Avalon	**USA - KY**
Nissan	Titan	**USA - MS**
Acura	MDA	**USA - OH**
Acura	TLX	**USA - OH**
Honda	Accord	**USA - OH**
Honda	CR-V	**USA - OH**
BMW	X-Series	**USA - SC**
VW	Passat	**USA - TN**
VW	Atlas	**USA - TN**

Source: U.S. News & World Report, Newsday, hotcars.com.

There are foreign automakers that assemble a higher percentage of their U.S.-sold vehicles in the U.S.than some American companies. While Lincoln only assembles 17 percent and Chrysler 33 percent of their U.S.-sold vehicles in the U.S., Acura assembles 71 percent of the vehicles it sells to the U.S.in the U.S., a striking difference—so much for "American."[98] And Acura isn't just a one-company exception. Sixty-one percent of Toyota's and 55 percent of Nissan's U.S.-sold vehicles are assembled in the U.S.[99] Returning to our original question: Which of these automobile manufacturers is the most "American"?

This phenomenon isn't confined to the automobile industry. In the aerospace industry, Boeing is building a manufacturing plant in China[100] that will deliver planes to serve the growing Chinese market. Conversely, the European consortium Airbus is now building planes at a factory in Alabama.[101] Ironic that an American company will employ Chinese workers to fulfill the growing demand of Chinese companies while a foreign company will employ American workers to capture a greater share of the American market. Even when China buys more "American" products, they increasingly may not be made in America.

"American-*made*" is becoming far more important than "buy American," as American companies increasingly make products outside the U.S. with non-American employees.

---

98 Johnson, "See Which Car Companies."

99 "Reality Check," BBC.com.

100 "Boeing Opens First Overseas Factory in China," CGTN.com, Sept. 27, 2017.

101 Alwyn Scott and Tim Hepher, "Aiming for U.S. Market, Airbus Delivers First U.S.-Made Jetliner," Reuters, April 25, 2016.

Global Trade Reality #5: Many iconic American products are made outside of America by foreign workers.

> "American-*made*" is becoming far more important than "buy American," as American companies increasingly make products outside the U.S. with non-American employees.

There are solutions for dealing with this myth—information. Information can be truly empowering.

Trade Solution #3: This is the same as Corporate Tax Solution #11. Packaging for products sold in America, regardless of the company nationality, prominently displays the percentage of employees (including subcontractors) utilized in the production of the products that are American-based.

Trade Solution #4: Create a ranking of the most patriotic companies selling goods and services in the U.S., regardless of nationality.

Rank the patriotism of each company based on the percentage of a company's employees that are American-based and the wages paid relative to its competitors.

> The enforcement mechanism of the free market, the choices consumers make, only works when the facts are easily accessible and widely known.

With this data and ranking, consumers will be able to identify which products utilize a higher percentage of American workers. Why is this necessary? The enforcement mechanism of the free market, the choices consumers make, only works when the facts are easily accessible and widely known. Only then is the enforcement mechanism of the free market more than a theory. Only then will the invisible hand of the free market have a visible impact.

Global Trade Myth #6: Americans will get all the high-tech jobs.

This myth is that other countries are only pursuing low-skill, low-wage jobs, leaving all the high-tech, high-skill, high-wage jobs for Americans. Really? General Electric committed to investing $2 billion in innovation and technology partnerships in China. This includes an $80 million innovation center in Chengdu and another in Xi' an,[102] the first in a series of innovation centers. These aren't shops to make soccer balls or Barbie dolls; these are innovation centers focusing on health care, technology, and transportation. Think service jobs aren't impacted? We only have to look to the world of finance to see that is not the case. When I worked in GE's commercial finance business, the company was using financial analysts in India rather than America to prepare the financial statements of companies it was considering lending money to.

General Electric is not alone in outsourcing high-technology investments and high-skill jobs. Microsoft has six innovation centers in China. Innovation centers are "...local hubs that provide resources and support for students and entrepreneurs, helping to accelerate the creation of new companies, jobs and growth of the local ecosystem."[103] Honeywell has also made major investments in China's innovation drive, establishing an aerospace academy in China.[104] According to Mark Howes, president of Honeywell

102 Richard Fu, "GE Opens Innovation Center in Chengdu," *Shanghai Daily*, May 30, 2012.

103 MicrosoftInnovationCenters.com.

104 "Honeywell Establishes China Aerospace Academy to Build Up Aviation Talents," Honeywell press release, Nov. 17, 2009.

Aerospace Asia-Pacific region, "Honeywell has dedicated substantial resources to support China's plans to grow its domestic aviation industry." Again, not exactly low-tech.[105] In the medical field, radiologists from outside the U.S.read 90 percent of X-rays taken in the U.S.[106] Competition within the technology sector from outside the U.S.is only likely to get more intense.

China's Plan for Technological Superiority and Dominance

China is making a concerted effort to dominate across the technology spectrum, announcing its "Made in China 2025" strategic plan. What does the plan entail? First, it is focused on upgrading its manufacturing capabilities to compete in innovation-related manufacturing as opposed to only undifferentiated mass manufacturing. Second, it is focused broadly on moving up the global production chain, providing more finished, high-value goods to the world. Third, "Made in China 2025" targets ten industries, and these aren't low-tech industries. They are advanced medical products, robotics, biopharma, aerospace, and information technology, among others.[107] The initiative is intended to grow domestic companies which will be competitive in the global marketplace, all with the purpose to replace use of foreign-sourced technology and

105 "Honeywell Helps Drive Chinese Aerospace Growth with Four Major Systems for New Passenger Aircraft," Honeywell press release, Nov. 19, 2010.

106 "Some 90% of Radiology Services in the U.S. Hospitals Are Outsourced," ZMEscience.com, Jan. 6, 2014.

107 "Made in China 2025," Center for Strategic and International Studies, June 1, 2015.

goods with domestically produced technology.[108] China is planning to expand beyond dominating low-cost manufacturing to dominating in industries more dependent on brains than brawn, and it is already well on its way.

> China already has the two most powerful supercomputers in the world.

China already has the two most powerful supercomputers in the world, the Sunway TaihuLight and Tianhe-2. The Sunway TaihuLight's processing capability is about equal to the combined processing capacity of the next ten fastest computers. More directly, as it relates to the U.S., it is 5.3 times faster than the fastest U.S. supercomputer. It is not just that China poured all its resources into two computers. China has 160 supercomputers, barely second to the U.S., with 168 supercomputers. China has turned its supercomputer achievements into super market-share growth. In 2011 Lenovo held 1 percent of the Chinese high-performance computing market; by 2016, its market share had skyrocketed to 34 percent. And China doesn't want domestic firms to stop there: China is targeting 60 percent market share of the high-performance computing market…by 2020. While China's high-performance computing market is expanding, U.S. companies "have little access to government bids," the greatest source of demand.[109] China's rapid technological gains is this generation's Sputnik moment, its wake-up call, that China's

108 "China's Pursuit of Dominance in Computing, Robotics, and Biotechnology," in "2017 Annual Report to Congress," U.S.-China Economic and Security Review Commission, Chapter 4, Section 1.

109 Ibid., 516, 517.

technology capability is gaining fast and even surpassing the U.S.in certain technological areas.

China is also making headway in areas beyond the realm of supercomputers. The world's largest floating solar power plant is in China, while China has announced plans to build a solar expressway on which vehicles will be able to be charged as they drive. It was a Chinese company, WinSun Decoration Design Engineering, not an American company, that built a ten-home village in one day using 3D printing and built what was, at the time, the world's tallest 3D-printed building.[110]

It seems China will only continue to expand its high-tech achievements. Huawei Technologies made more patent applications in 2016 than any other company in the world. Transforming patents into products will be aided by rapidly expanding venture capital investment with $77 billion in venture capital funding between 2014 and 2016, as compared to a mere $12 billion the prior two years. China is already well on its way with an estimated one-third of the world's "unicorns," private companies with $1 billion-plus valuations, domiciled in China. These include Da Jiang Innovations Science and Technology (DJI), which already commands 70 percent of the consumer drone market. Additionally, China was responsible for one-third

China is already well on its way with an estimated one-third of the world's "unicorns," private companies with $1 billion-plus valuations, domiciled in China.

110 Cecilia Zhang, "Nine Amazing Examples of High-Tech Innovation in China," *ChinaDaily.com*, March 6, 2018.

of the world's nearly 300,000 robots purchased in 2016.[111] China is also quickly becoming a nation that is developing its own technology. According to Jing Ulrich vice chairman of Asia Pacific, JPMorgan Chase, "China is changing from the so-called copycat nation to innovation nation."[112]

Global Trade Reality #6: Countries including China are increasingly focusing on the same high-skill, high-wage industries and jobs we were supposed to rely on to offset the lower-skilled jobs already lost to them.

Global Trade Myth #7: It's okay if we send our jobs overseas. American workers will get all the higher-paying jobs.

While this is a comforting theory that conveniently alleviates concerns relating to sending jobs overseas, it doesn't match reality. As we just saw, we have significant and increasing competition in high-tech, high-wage industries. Second, this myth assumes that those losing jobs have the skills to qualify for higher-paying jobs, such as the high-tech jobs we keep hearing will replace the lower-tech jobs sent overseas. However, as we will see later, not all displaced workers have those skills. Third, to make matters worse, rather than training the displaced workers for those jobs, some would like to further liberalize immigration for higher-skilled workers, increasing competition for the higher-paying jobs touted as the safety valve for those watching their manufacturing jobs migrate overseas.

111 Chandler, "Why China."

112 Choudhury, "Reporter's Notebook."

From a Nation of Makers to Order Takers

From 2000 until 2017, U.S. manufacturing employment declined by more than 4.6 million, from more than 17 million to about 12.5 million jobs. Not to worry, leisure and hospitality employment increased during the same 2000-2017 period by 4.2 million, from just under 12 million to more than 16 million jobs,[113] just about the same number of manufacturing jobs lost. We went from a nation of makers to a nation of order takers.

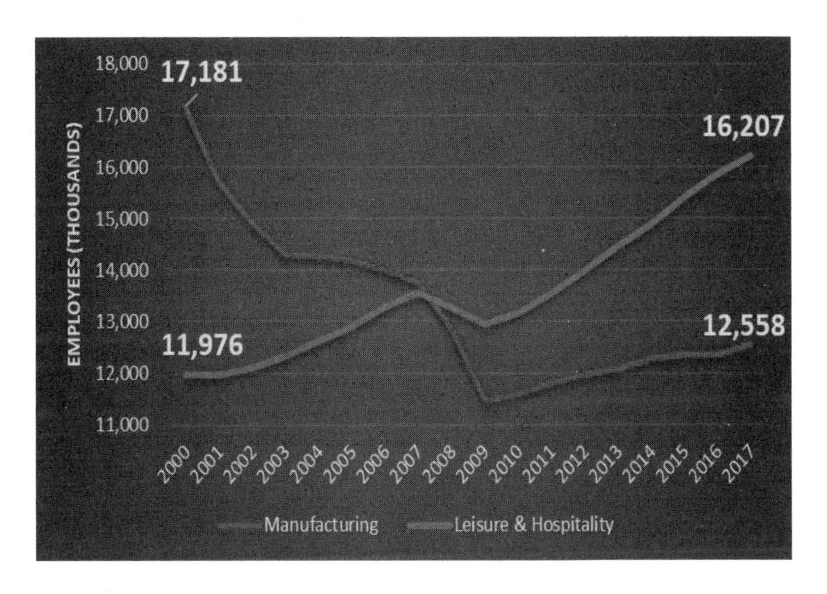

Source: Federal Reserve Bank of St. Louis

This has serious ramifications for the U.S. economy, especially the 70 percent of GDP growth that is driven by consumer purchases.

113 Federal Reserve Bank of St. Louis.

Leisure and hospitality wages are one-third less than manufacturing wages, $13.60 an hour versus $21.21 an hour. Assuming forty hours a week and fifty-two weeks of work, while manufacturing pays more than $44,000 a year on average, leisure and hospitality pays $28,000[114] a year—$16,000 less a year. Significant portions of manufacturing workers also made their way into other lower-paying retail sectors. From 2000-2007, more than 40 percent[115] of displaced manufacturing workers went into the retail, administration support and waste management, and wholesale trade sectors. These aren't exactly the types of jobs that were promised to workers, as their jobs were being freely sent overseas.

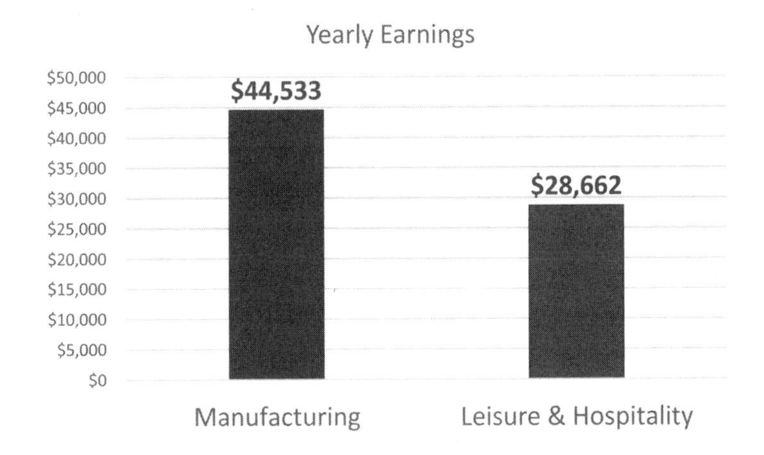

Source: Federal Reserve Bank of St. Louis

114 Federal Reserve Bank of St. Louis

115 Cristina Tello-Trillo, Justin Pierce, and Peter K. Schott, "Where Did All the U.S. Manufacturing Workers Go? Evidence from U.S. Matched Employer-Employee Data." October 10, 2017.

What happened? While we only have data through 2014, we know that, from 2000 through 2014, the number of U.S. manufacturing establishments declined by more than 78,000, or more than 22 percent. This compares to an increase of more than 8,000 manufacturing establishments during the prior fourteen-year period.[116]

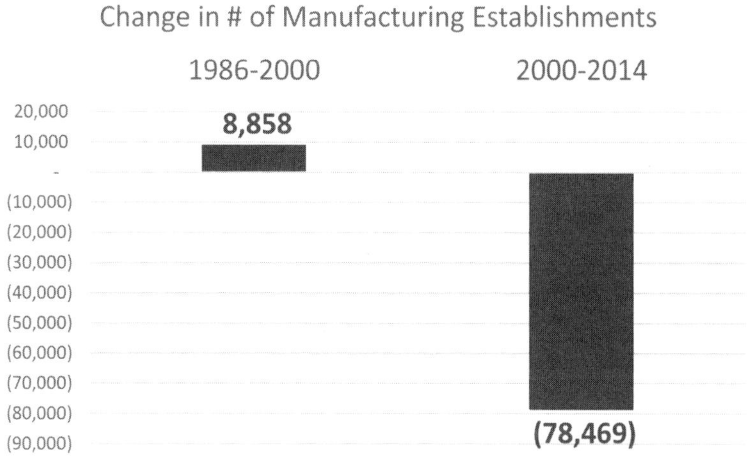

Change in # of Manufacturing Establishments

1986-2000 2000-2014

20,000
10,000
-
(10,000)
(20,000)
(30,000)
(40,000)
(50,000)
(60,000)
(70,000)
(80,000)
(90,000)

8,858
(78,469)

Source: U.S. Census Bureau

Some say the majority of the decline in manufacturing employment and establishments was due to automation, not global trade. Even if that were the case, that is all the more reason to do everything we can to minimize the losses of manufacturing employment due to globalization. The impact of automation on manufacturing

116 U.S. Census Bureau.

> The impact of automation on manufacturing or any job should be a call to action to limit the losses due to globalization, not a justification for continuing to follow trade policies which send more manufacturing jobs overseas.

or any job should be a call to action to limit the losses due to globalization, not a justification for continuing to follow trade policies which send more manufacturing jobs overseas. Still, others may say there were increases in higher-paying occupations from 2000-2017, like professional and business services. While some have gotten jobs in those fields, as we will see, the jobs often weren't higher-paying and were sometimes lower-paying. The other higher-paying jobs held out as hope for the displaced manufacturing employees require advanced degrees, something not all employee manufacturing employees have. So, while there were jobs created in other higher-paying fields, they require different skills and degrees.

Global Trade Reality #7: Displaced American workers don't always get higher-paying jobs.

Global Trade Myth #8: Concern over trade deficits is antiquated—they don't matter.

This is an increasingly common myth that is used to try and discredit attempts to reduce the United States' massive trade deficit. The argument is that trade deficits are actually good because they are the result of consumers buying more, which is only possible when consumers are doing well financially. First, this doesn't change the fact that, as the trade deficit increases, we are increasingly indebted to the rest of the world. Second, implicit in this argument is the assumption that *where* the goods Americans are buying come from is fixed, so when Americans buy more, the goods deficits can only increase. Here's a thought: if the U.S. imported less and made more, when Americans consumed more, the deficit wouldn't increase as much. The fact that trade deficits rise when consumers are buying more doesn't magically make the deficits a positive. That is the equivalent of a business that loses money on every product it sells, believing the problem is solved when they sell more.

The next specious argument used to downplay trade deficits is that trade deficits are merely an accounting function. Of course, they are an accounting function! They account for how much we buy from the rest of the world, versus how much the rest of the world buys from us, and the accounting shows that we are increasingly on the losing side!

> The fact that trade deficits rise when consumers are buying more doesn't magically make trade deficits a positive. That is the equivalent of a business that loses money on every product it sells, believing the problem is solved when they sell more.

The third and perhaps most insulting attempt to minimize the importance of reducing our trade deficits is that trade deficits can be a good thing. How? Because they indicate we are saving less than other countries, instead investing more in capital goods, which will increase our productivity and thus, long-term income and wealth. Sounds plausible until you look at the facts and see that, in 2017, capital goods only represented a small portion of our imports, just over

27 percent.[117] Said another way, nearly 75 percent of our imports were comprised of noncapital goods, goods that decreased our wealth, including toys, trinkets, and all the items you would generally find in a Bed Bath & Beyond. But let's just say, for discussion purposes, that all the goods America imports are investment in nature. What if, for example, the robotics we import from Japan and Germany were instead made in the U.S.? We would still be investing and both reducing the trade deficit as well as increasing U.S. employment.

There is also an idea that trade deficits are fine and have no negative effects, such as a decrease in manufacturing jobs. I think the chart below showing the increasing goods deficit and concurrent reduction in manufacturing employment is self-explanatory and too clear to be chalked up to a coincidence or entirely due to automation.

> Nearly 75 percent of our imports in 2017 were comprised of noncapital goods, goods that decreased our wealth, including toys and trinkets, not capital goods that would increase the country's wealth.

117 "Real Imports of Goods by Principal End-Use Category," U.S. Census Bureau.

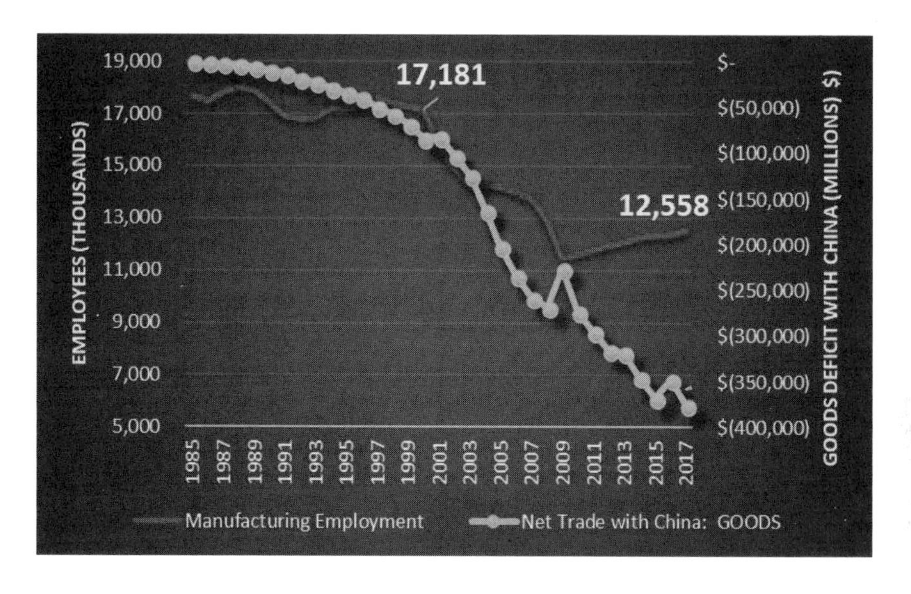

Source: Federal Reserve Bank of St. Louis, U.S. Census Bureau

Global Trade Reality #8: Trade deficits do matter.

Global Trade Myth #9: When jobs in America are shipped overseas, 100 percent of the cost savings is passed on to American consumers.

Perhaps the foundational justification for sending jobs overseas, importing more goods, and never even questioning today's trading environment is that they improve the standard of living for Americans. The argument goes like this: Sending jobs overseas is okay and actually good for Americans, because it makes goods cheaper, increasing our standard of living. However, a key assumption in this is that 100 percent of the cost savings associated with moving production overseas is passed on to consumers. In reality, companies move production to countries with lower costs primarily to make more profits, not to offer American consumers lower-priced goods. I'm not saying that is a good or bad thing. What is bad is naively assuming that 100 percent of the cost savings is passed on to consumers.

Global Trade Reality #9: Not all labor savings are passed on to consumers.

This reality significantly weakens the argument for sending jobs overseas based on the assumption that it increases the standard of living. The next trade reality weakens the argument further.

Global Trade Myth #10: Only price determines whether a good is cheap or expensive.

The price of a good is only one part of what determines how cheap or expensive a good is. The other half is the income of the purchaser. Let me give an example.

> The price of a good is only one part of what determines how cheap or expensive a good is. The other half is the income of the purchaser.

A friend went to a store with his young son. His son wanted to buy something, and he asked his father how much it was. The price was one dollar. Pulling the change of out his pocket and realizing he only had fifty cents, his son exclaimed, "That's expensive!" Whether an item is expensive depends both on the price of the good *and* the income of the purchaser. Those "cheap" goods made outside the U.S. aren't cheap when you don't have a job or are getting paid less. There is an additional cost that is not included when looking solely at the price of a good made outside the U.S.: welfare costs. If you add in the costs of welfare and other government programs that are used to supplement the income of those whose jobs were sent overseas and either don't have a job or are now working at lower wages and, thus, qualify for welfare, the price of those "cheap" goods made outside the U.S. increases further.

An example of this is found in the steel industry. The San Francisco-Oakland Bay Bridge and New York's Verrazzano-Narrows Bridge projects both used Chinese-made steel. Looking at the price of the steel alone would give a very different picture than if other key costs were included. These include American jobs lost, wages lost, and the demand for welfare created by having individuals who could have been working in U.S.-based steel plants making the steel, instead of working at lower-paying jobs or not working at all, thus, qualifying for welfare. Add in the fact that, as we saw in Global Trade Myth #3, other countries don't make production decisions based on return on investment but on how many people they will employ, and we can see that the cost of having Chinese companies make the steel is higher than just the price of the steel. And remember, it is not just those whose jobs were sent overseas who are impacted. Because the demand for labor is reduced when a job is sent overseas, overall wages will not grow as fast, as more people are competing for fewer jobs.

Additionally, while the cost of some goods has been constrained by having other countries make goods, pricing of bigger-ticket items including education, housing, and health care have significantly outpaced income growth. We may be getting cheaper TVs, iPhones, and cars but education, housing, and

> Are cheap imported electronics and toys worth sacrificing the ability to afford education, housing, and health care?

health care costs are growing out of reach for an increasing number of Americans. Are cheap imported electronics and toys worth sacrificing the ability to afford education, housing, and health care?

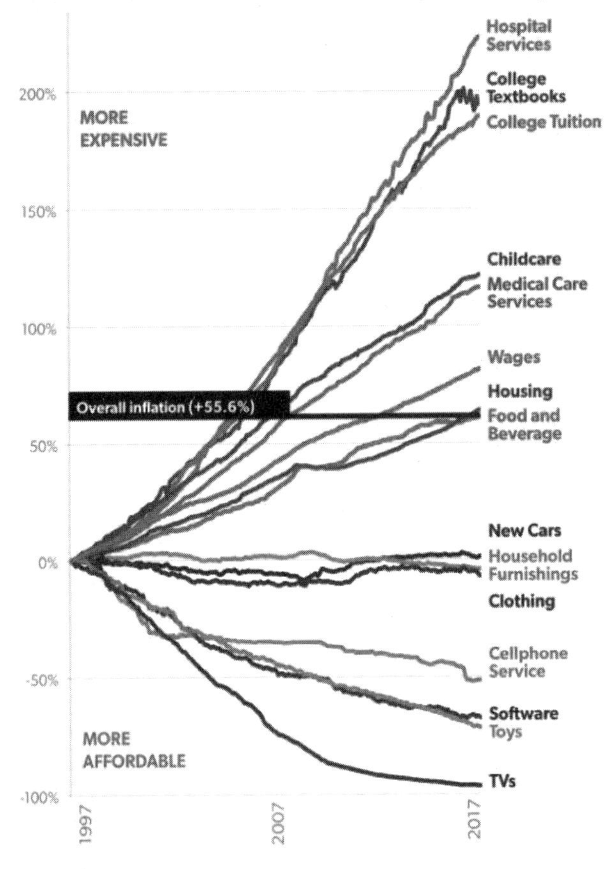

Source: American Enterprise Institute using Bureau of Labor Statistics data

Global Trade Reality #10: The price of an imported good is only one part of the cost of making more goods overseas vs. domestically.

Now, does this mean all goods should be made in America? Of course not. What it does mean is that all costs resulting from making a good overseas versus in the U.S. should be considered.

Trade Solution #5: All costs to the American taxpayer of the government, federal, state, and local, for procuring goods overseas versus in America, including lost American wages and associated taxes, health care benefits, unemployment costs, welfare, and other government assistance are factored in when governments weigh whether to buy American-made products or foreign-made products. This will ensure the shareholders of USA Inc. get a better return on their taxpayer dollars.

Global Trade Myth #11: It's always best to have other countries make things if they can make them cheaper.

This may be the most deceptive and damaging trade myth. Why? Because it cloaks itself in the credentials of a popular but flawed theory called "absolute advantage," to justify sending more and more jobs overseas.

A key consideration in whether it makes sense to have other countries make goods we could make is the following:

> Do we have enough jobs, of equal pay, to replace the jobs sent overseas? If we don't, it makes no sense to send even more jobs overseas.

Absolute advantage states that a country should produce what it can produce more cheaply than other countries and buy from other countries that which they can produce more cheaply. Adam Smith summarized absolute advantage, stating,

"If a foreign country can supply us with a commodity cheaper than we ourselves can make it, better to buy it of them...."[118] His faith in the universal truth of this theory was so great that he went on to state, "As long as one country has those advantages (resources allowing to produce more cheaply), and the other one wants them (goods), it will *always* be more advantageous....[119] The broader idea or goal of absolute advantage is to concentrate your resources, people, and raw materials on what you can make more cheaply than other countries and buy from others what you cannot. Doing so is supposed to increase the standard of living for the country. However, as we saw, price alone does not determine whether a good is cheap or expensive. Thus, price alone should not determine whether we should produce something or have another country produce it. Most importantly, when considering having others make things we could be making, we also need to consider whether we have enough jobs of at least equal pay to replace the jobs sent overseas. Critically, absolute advantage assumes we have the luxury of letting other countries produce goods we could have made, but we know that is not always the case. If you doubt this, just look at Flint, Michigan, Gary, Indiana, or any of a number of other former thriving manufacturing cities. We not only didn't have equal-paying jobs to replace those lost overseas, it was not unusual to have no jobs for those who lost their jobs. This is shown by the declining labor force participation rates[120] among the occupations most impacted by global trade and in the towns

118 Adam Smith, *The Wealth of Nations*, Book IV, Chapter II, 478.

119 Ibid., 480.

120 Layman's definition: The size of the labor force compared to the size of the working-age population.

most impacted by absolute advantage taken too far.

> Absolute advantage assumes we have the luxury of letting other countries produce goods we could have made, but we know that is not always the case. If you doubt this, just look at Flint, Michigan, Gary, Indiana, or any of a number of other former thriving manufacturing cities.

Technical definition from the Bureau of Labor Statistics: The percentage of the non-institutional working-age population, sixteen years and older, that is in the labor force, meaning either working or looking for work.[121]

Sending more jobs overseas when we don't have enough good-paying jobs to replace the jobs lost makes no sense. How crazy is it? Imagine you are the shareholder of a domestic company and the CEO sends out a letter giving notice that the company is going to stop producing one of its products and will, instead, buy the product from another company. The CEO goes on to explain that this makes sense because the other company can make the goods more cheaply. Sounds good, right? There is a catch: The domestic company does not have work for the employees who used to produce what will now be produced overseas and, most importantly, the company has agreed to continue to pay the workers a minimum standard of living for life. So the company is paying another company to produce the goods, while still paying its workers who are no longer producing the goods. In this example, America is the company

121 "How the Government Measures Unemployment: Labor Force Participation Rate," U.S. Bureau of Labor Statistics, https://www.bls.gov/cps/cps_htgm.htm#definitions.

and you and I are shareholders and, importantly, you and I pay for the laid-off employees through welfare—we are subsidizing the company's profits.

> We are trading wages for welfare checks. Other countries increasingly produce things while we increasingly produce welfare checks.

What has this blind faith in an absolute advantage led to in this country? We are paying other countries to make things that our working-age citizens could be making, all while paying the laid-off workers in the form of welfare checks and other forms of government assistance—*we are trading wages for welfare checks.* Do we want that to be our economic policy—other countries increasingly produce things while we increasingly produce welfare checks? No. Going back to our company illustration, no CEO would pay another company to make things when it has spare capacity for which it is still paying. Yet that is often what is happening when jobs are sent overseas: We pay for the goods twice, once to the other country and a second time through welfare checks.

Global Trade Reality #11: Price alone does not determine whether we should have other countries produce goods that Americans could produce. Whether we have enough jobs of equal pay for the employees whose jobs were sent overseas is the key.

When we buy into this myth that it's always best to have other countries make things if they can make them cheaper, we are simply trading wages for welfare checks, like we're doing today. It doesn't have to be that way. We can do better, and it begins with an *"all of the above"* jobs policy—because we need all of the good-paying jobs. How to do that?

Trade Solution #6: When evaluating the merits of having other countries make things we are or could be making, assess whether we have an equal number of jobs that pay at least as much.

Global Trade Myth #12: Global trade agreements are only about trade.

Have you ever wondered why U.S. automakers had such limited access to Japan's auto market for years, while Japanese automakers seemed to have unlimited access to our market? Or consider this: Why are our tariffs often significantly lower than the tariffs of other countries we trade with? Were our negotiators really that much worse than the negotiators of other countries? American foreign policy has been hijacking trade policy since World War II with trade agreements driven more by foreign policy objectives than trade policy objectives. Trade agreements were used by every president since WWII, both Republican and Democrat, to advance foreign policy objectives, all at the expense of American industries and jobs. Foreign countries were given highly favorable trade terms, including lower tariffs, while we faced higher tariffs, strict quotas, and other protectionist measures, limiting our access to foreign markets. This was done to limit Soviet expansionism after WWII, including through the rebuilding of the economies of Germany, Japan, and Italy to secure their alliance with the West, limiting the expansion potential of the Soviet Union.[122] At the time, the U.S. had a trade surplus. I know, hard to imagine in today's environment. It was a very different world with imports during the 1940s and '50s comprising 4 percent of U.S.GDP[123] as compared to 12

122 Eckes, Opening America's Market, 157.

123 Ibid., 158.

percent of GDP in 2017. By 2017, the U.S.no longer had a trade surplus but a trade deficit in goods and services of nearly $800 billion.[124]

After WWII, the U.S. was the world's global trading champ, not the chump like today. This led to an overconfidence for which we are paying today. In an ominous sign of this overconfidence, President Harry Truman himself said, "...our workingmen need no longer fear, as they were justified in the past, the competition of foreign workers."[125] During the early stages of the growing fear of Soviet influence, the U.S. engaged in both unilateral tariff reductions and use of U.S. government resources to actually promote imports. Yes, imports.[126] To mollify domestic economic interests, so-called trade assistance programs were put in place. These programs, with their components of unemployment benefits and job retraining programs, were the forerunners of what I previously outlined as our policy of producing welfare checks, while countries like China produce products. The prioritization of foreign policy over domestic economic interests continued under Truman's successor, Dwight Eisenhower. Eisenhower went so far as to blatantly and unequivocally state his bias to congressional leaders: "All problems of local industry pale into insignificance in relation to the world crisis."[127] While the fear of Communism would supersede domestic economic factors in the Eisenhower administration, former President Hoover made the following prophetic statement in 1953: "Thousands of villages and towns would be deprived of their employment. Their

124 U.S. Bureau of Economic Analysis and U.S. Census Bureau.

125 Eckes, 158.

126 Ibid., 165.

127 Ibid., 167.

schools, churches and skills would be greatly decimated."[128] Despite these misgivings, utilizing trade policy to contain Soviet expansion continued not only during the Eisenhower administration, but into President John F. Kennedy's administration, which used trade to unify Europe as a bulwark against Soviet expansion—new administration, same foreign policy priorities. This was not done out of ignorance. The Kennedy administration knew leveraging trade policy in the pursuit of foreign policy objectives would have detrimental impacts on certain U.S. industries, even telling British officials that the process would be painful and admitting that trade assistance programs were not likely to help much in reality.[129] Adding insult to injury, Kennedy's successor, Lyndon Johnson, failed to secure access to Japanese markets or gains in agricultural trade with the European Economic Community at the end of the Kennedy Round negotiations despite materially lowering U.S. tariffs. The Johnson administration chose achieving an agreement over achieving its trade objectives.[130] How far from the objectives did the final agreement stray? So much so that the trade representative for President Johnson's successor, Richard Nixon, told him, "The Japanese took advantage of this situation...."[131] Despite this, Nixon continued the practice of advancing foreign policy objectives at the expense of trade policy and domestic industry. Nixon used trade as a means to foreign policy ends. This included dangling the potential granting of Most Favored Nation status to the Soviet Union as well as starting the process which would eventually lead to

128 Ibid., 168.

129 Ibid., 185, 186.

130 Ibid., 196.

131 Ibid., 200, 202.

the granting of Most Favored Nation status to China in 1980.[132] It didn't take long for the negative effects of the Kennedy Round and Nixon's actions to be felt.

From 1893 to 1967, the U.S. had a surplus in merchandise trade with the rest of the world: For seventy-four years, we sold more goods to the world than were sold to the U.S. Beginning in 1968, this changed drastically, with trade deficits in goods becoming the norm. Why? While tariffs were reduced, they weren't always reduced to equal levels. U.S. tariffs on automobiles were reduced to 3 percent, in contrast to Japanese, UK, and European Economic Community automobile tariffs, which ranged from 10-15 percent—three to five times U.S. automobile tariffs. Additionally, non-tariff barriers including subsidies, quotas, and license agreements were used to constrain U.S. exports, despite reduced tariffs on U.S. products.[133] Not coincidentally, from 1968 to 1969, automobile imports nearly doubled and foreign automobile suppliers saw their U.S. market share more than double, from 7.2 percent in the years preceding the Kennedy Round tariff cuts, to more than 15 percent in the early 1970s.[134] On a macro level, U.S. exports as a percentage of industrialized countries' exports shrank precipitously from 28 percent in 1960 to 20 percent in 1973.[135] Unsurprisingly, manufacturing employment growth plateaued in 1969 and began to decline, while real manufacturing wage growth largely disappeared in the 1970s and subsequently began to decline.[136] Whereas

132 Ibid., 211.
133 Ibid., 203-205.
134 Ibid., 208.
135 Ibid., 179.
136 Ibid., 217.

the Kennedy Round may have been effective in advancing foreign policy objectives, it clearly had a detrimental impact on exports and domestic industries, sowing the seeds of heightened industry dislocations that would occur in the 1980s and 1990s.[137]

The policy of using trade in the service of advancing foreign policy objectives continues today. President Trump wrote in a tweet, "I explained to the President of China that a trade deal with the U.S. will be far better for them if they solve the North Korean problem!" This is simply a continuation of many years of presidents, of both political parties, using trade policy in the service of foreign policy.

> From 1893 to 1967, the U.S.had a surplus in merchandise trade with the rest of the world: For seventy-four years, we sold more goods to the world than were sold to the U.S.

We can debate the merits of using trade agreements to achieve foreign policy objectives. What cannot be debated is that, when this has occurred in the past, there have been negative domestic economic effects.

Global Trade Reality # 12: Trade agreements are as much about foreign policy as they are global trade.

Big and Small Businesses: Very Different Views of Global Trade

Large and small businesses can have very different perspectives regarding global trade. Big businesses generally place a much higher value on accessing foreign markets than small businesses.

137 Ibid., 218.

Why? Once a large business has saturated the U.S.market, it needs to expand into foreign markets to maintain its growth rate. The U.S.only needs so many Starbucks and Dunkin Donuts locations. Conversely, small businesses generally don't have as great a need to expand outside the U.S., because they have expansion opportunities within the U.S. This can result in big businesses lobbying for trade agreements that have unequal and unfavorable trade terms for the U.S., in return for gaining or increasing access to foreign markets. Conversely, small businesses may place a higher value on not introducing additional competition into an already highly competitive marketplace. This can create a significant disconnect between what is good in terms of trade agreements for big businesses and the small business owners selling mostly to U.S. customers. This is a critical distinction, as it is one reason why some companies may support a trade agreement while others don't.

14. ADDITIONAL SOLUTIONS FOR WINNING THE GAME OF GLOBAL TRADE

Trade Solution #7: Companies selling goods and services in the U.S. publish quarterly how many American-based jobs they eliminated, how many were sent overseas or subcontracted to overseas subcontractors, the wages lost, benefits lost, and the welfare collected by the American employees who lost their jobs. Companies also publish how many jobs they created in America, the wages gained, benefits gained, and reduction in welfare. Then we can get a real accounting of the impact of outsourcing versus hiring in America.

Rather than focusing on the nationality of a company, use the data above to instead focus on how many jobs a company creates in America, what percentage of its workforce is based in the U.S., the level of wages it pays, and the health insurance benefits it provides. The importance of focusing on what each company is contributing to our workforce, not the nationality, cannot be overstated.

The importance of focusing on what each company is contributing to our work-force, not the nationality, cannot be overstated

Trade Solution #8: Create a patriotic ranking of American companies.

Rank the patriotism of companies selling goods in the U.S. Determine the ranking based on the percentage of each company's employees used in producing the goods sold goods in the U.S. and the wages paid relative to competitors.

Trade Solution #9: Similar to Corporate Tax Solution numbers 3, 4, and 5, tie company tax rates to the rate of job creation in America. This will provide an incentive for companies to keep more jobs in America.

Trade Solution #10: If foreign governments require companies selling goods in their countries to make the goods in their country, we do the same.

That's not protectionist; that's finally leveling the playing field. It's asserting our independence from being every other country's global trading chump.

Trade Solution #11: Eliminate Most Favored Nation status.

Most Favored Nation status (MFN) entitles countries with U.S.MFN status to receive the same concessions that any other country has received. For example, if the U.S. were to eliminate its tariffs on Canadian steel, then every other

It's asserting our independence from being every other country's global trading chump.

country with MFN would also have tariffs on its steel eliminated. The problem is that while the U.S. may have eliminated tariffs on Canadian steel in return for a trade concession from Canada, other countries with favored status would have given nothing and still benefited from the elimination of the steel tariff. As a result, countries with this would get a free ride. This eliminates the opportunities for the U.S.to gain something in return, as it significantly reduces the U.S. negotiating power by reducing the number of items available to use in negotiations.

15. NAFTA IMPACT: DEPENDS ON WHO YOU ASK

The North American Free Trade Agreement (NAFTA) was highly controversial and hotly debated. Proponents and opponents alike have produced studies analyzing the effects of NAFTA on the American economy, employment, composition of employment, wages, specific industries, jobs, and geographies. Unfortunately, these studies are often meant more to support the position of the author(s) than to present a balanced, objective picture of the effects. Let's start with a pro-NAFTA paper, move to an anti-NAFTA paper, and finish with what is a more balanced paper.

Those looking to build the case for NAFTA and specific facts and figures to be used in talking points will find the U.S. Chamber of Commerce's presentation, *The Facts on NAFTA: Assessing Two Decades of Gains in Trade, Growth, and Jobs,* a useful resource. The primary arguments of the Chamber's presentation are:

- Trading activity among the U.S., Canada, and Mexico increased.
- Eighty-eight percent of manufacturing job losses were due to automation.

- Five million American jobs are the result of the increase in trade among the three countries.
- Manufacturing employment increased by 800,000 in the first four years following implementation of NAFTA.
- Manufacturing employment peaked in 1979 well before NAFTA.
- Prices for consumer goods decreased, benefiting consumers.

Let's take these one by one.

First, it is true that trade in goods and services among the three countries increased significantly, going from $337 billion in 1993 to $1.4 trillion in 2014. However, increased trade among the three countries does not automatically mean the U.S. was a net beneficiary. As we saw in Myth #8, while some may try to argue that trade deficits don't matter, the reality is that they do, and during the 1993-2014 period referenced, USA Inc.'s trade deficit in goods with both Canada and Mexico increased. In 1993, the U.S. trade goods deficit with Canada was less than $11 billion; in 2014, it was more than $36 billion, a tripling of the trade deficit in goods. Turning to trade in goods with Mexico, USA Inc. went from a $1.7 billion goods trade surplus in 1993 to a goods deficit of nearly $57 billion in 2014, a massive shift to the negative. Yes, during this same time frame, U.S. exports of services increased. However, as a later paper we will review highlights, service jobs generally pay less than manufacturing jobs. Importantly, we will see later in Section IV, Expanding the American Middle Class, that it is these higher-paying manufacturing jobs which are declining in the U.S., not service jobs. This leads into the next point made by the Chamber of Commerce paper in support of NAFTA: 88 percent of jobs lost in manufacturing are due to automation.

The Chamber of Commerce presentation cites a study by Ball State University, *The Myth and Reality of Manufacturing in the U.S.*, which concluded that 88 percent of the manufacturing jobs lost from 2000 to 2010 were due to productivity gains. First, the paper also states, "Losses in productivity and trade varied dramatically by sectors, with those *sectors most heavily exposed to international competition suffering the greatest declines.*" This is kind of an important point when examining the effects of a trade agreement that significantly increased imports. It is, at best, odd that it was omitted from the Chamber's paper. Second, is 88 percent of manufacturing jobs lost due to productivity gains supposed to make the significant goods deficit increase with Canada and Mexico any less damaging? As I said before, if automation is ransacking manufacturing jobs, the normal response would be, "Let's ensure we are doing everything else we can in the areas we can control, including in our trade policy, to maintain manufacturing jobs." Yet the Chamber seems to instead be saying, "Automation is the real culprit in manufacturing job losses, so don't worry about job losses resulting from trade with NAFTA." With that kind of thinking influencing our trade policy, small wonder we are the world's global trading chumps. Third, other papers attribute less impact due to productivity, but the Chamber doesn't mention those. Fourth, the Chamber fails to mention both that the Ball State paper estimates that, from 2000 to 2010, 1.4 million to 1.7 million jobs were lost due to increased imports, and that the Ball State paper states, "Exports lead to higher levels of domestic production and employment, while imports reduce domestic production and employment." Given the significant and increased goods deficits with Canada and Mexico, it is, again, odd not to mention this quote. This omission goes from odd to suspect, since the Chamber's third point in support of NAFTA is that 5 million jobs were created because of increased trading activity, yet they don't mention the Ball State estimate of how many jobs were lost due to increased imports.

The Chamber's next fact in support of NAFTA is an estimated 800,000 increase in manufacturing jobs in the first four years following NAFTA. Why did they choose 1994-1998? Why not 1994 to 2001 as an example? It is worth noting that in 1994, the U.S. had only recently gotten out of a recession and manufacturing was coming off a near-cycle low, meaning that manufacturing employment would increase with some companies merely hiring back employees they had fired during the recession. If the analysis had been from 1994 to right before the next recession in 2001 the increase in manufacturing jobs from 1994 would have been less than 250,000, which is very low, considering, again, that the starting point was near an economic trough. Last, the Chamber fails to mention that the Ball State paper estimates that, from 2000 to 2010, 5.6 million manufacturing jobs were lost.

The Chamber next notes that U.S. manufacturing employment peaked in 1979, fifteen years before NAFTA. The inference is that, because manufacturing was already on the decline before NAFTA, it didn't have much, if anything, to do with the decline in manufacturing jobs. Add in the 800,000 manufacturing jobs added from 1994-1998 and it leaves the audience with the idea that NAFTA increased manufacturing employment, an impression benefiting from the omission of key facts and statements from the same paper cited by the Chamber.

The Chamber's last point in support of NAFTA is that it lowered prices for consumers. While this is true for certain products, it is not for all products. As we saw in myths number 7 and 10, a) those whose jobs were shipped overseas don't always get jobs paying more or even the same amount as the jobs they lost, instead having to take jobs paying less; and b) price is only one component of whether a good is cheap or expensive, with lower-paying replacement jobs making the skyrocketing costs of other items such as rent, education, and health care even more painful for consumers. It is one thing to be able to buy a cheaper air conditioner, and another to be making less at the same time your rent is increasing.

Those looking to build a case against NAFTA citing specific facts and figures to be used in talking points will find Public Citizen's paper, *NAFTA's 20-Year Legacy and the Fate of the Trans-Pacific Partnership,* a good source. While the paper includes many arguments in building a case against NAFTA, the primary arguments relate to the increase in trade deficits between the U.S. and both Canada and Mexico, job losses attributable to NAFTA, and a NAFTA-related reduction in consumer purchasing power of $3,300.

First, yes, the U.S. has had a much higher trade deficit with Canada and Mexico subsequent to the passage of NAFTA. However, Public Citizen fails to mention the important fact that other factors such as currency movements, including the Mexican peso crisis, also contributed to the increase in deficits.

The second argument made in opposition to NAFTA is that 1 million net jobs were lost due to NAFTA from 1994 to 2004. First, while it is net job creation that is most important, it failed to note that, despite this net job loss, an estimated 1 million jobs were created due to increased NAFTA-related exports. This would have shown that jobs were both destroyed *and* created because of NAFTA, rather than potentially creating the perception that no jobs were created because of NAFTA. Additionally, the Public Citizen paper notes that from 1994 through 2013, nearly double the time frame of the estimated 1 million job losses, the number of workers receiving Trade Adjustment Assistance (TAA) due to NAFTA import- and factory relocation-related job losses was 845,000. While Public Citizen rightly notes the caveats in using the number of employees receiving TAA, the gap between the 845,000 qualifying for TAA from 1994-2013 and the significantly higher 2 million estimated NAFTA-related job losses in nearly half the time (1994-2004) reveals how much uncertainty there is in the actual impact of NAFTA on job losses and gains.

The third Public Citizen argument is that consumer purchasing power declined, contrary to most arguments in support of NAFTA and free trade. Citing a paper by the Center for Economic and Policy Research, *Will New Trade Gains Make Us Rich*, Public Citizen estimated that workers earning the median annual wage of $27,500 saw a $3,300 or 12 percent reduction in purchasing power because of NAFTA, even when accounting for the reduced price of consumer goods. This is based first on the Center for Economic and Policy Research's paper estimate of trade-related wage losses of 1.6 percent to 2.4 percent, a far cry from the 12 percent Public Citizen used. Second, multiple other sources estimate a net gain in consumer purchasing power from trade, including a paper by former President Barack Obama's White House titled, "The Economic Benefits of Trade," which estimated trade added 29 percent to consumer purchasing power, versus an economy without trade. Given the wide range in underlying assumptions regarding wage losses and impact of trade on final consumer purchasing power, this is far from a settled subject, which Public Citizen could have conveyed, rather than presenting it as a settled question.

Those looking for a balanced perspective on the impacts of NAFTA are advised to read both the Chamber of Commerce and Public Citizen materials in the same manner as when you are considering buying a car and you want to know everything about it: Ask the salesperson for the competing brand that makes its car superior to the car you are considering. Alternatively, a paper, "Looking for Local Labor Market Effects of NAFTA," written by John McLaren of the University of Virginia and Shushanik Hakobyan of Fordham University, provides a useful perspective. It presents an evaluation of the wage effects of NAFTA and analyzes the effects based on industries, geographies, and subsets of workers. Evaluating the effects of NAFTA at this more granular level revealed greater negative effects than previous analyses conducted at a broader, national level.

The authors concluded that NAFTA lowered wage growth most for blue-collar workers, workers in industries facing direct competition from NAFTA imports, and workers in towns with elevated concentrations of industries exposed to NAFTA import competition. However, the most striking finding of the paper is that even workers in non-tradeable industries, industries not competing with imports, suffered declines in wages if the workers were in towns exposed to NAFTA-related increases in imports.[138] The author

138 John McLaren and Shushanik Hakobyan, "Looking for Local Labor Market Effects of NAFTA," National Bureau of Economic Research Working Paper No. 16535, January 2012, 22.

hypothesizes that this is both because workers losing jobs in the tradable industries increase competition for the remaining jobs in non-tradable industries and because of the reduced incomes resulting from those who lost jobs due to increased foreign competition. NAFTA negatively impacted not just workers in industries facing import competition and reduced tariffs, but all workers in towns with elevated vulnerability levels to NAFTA. The author notes that a high school dropout living in an apparel- and footwear-dependent town in South Carolina but not employed in a tradeable industry such as at a local restaurant would still suffer greater negative wage growth effects than a worker in a similar job in College Park, Maryland, which had a limited number of NAFTA-exposed jobs.[139] A white-collar worker employed in an industry with no NAFTA exposure in a town with most companies having limited exposure to NAFTA import competition would fare the best.

NAFTA negatively impacted not just workers in industries facing import competition and reduced tariffs but all workers in towns with elevated vulnerability levels to NAFTA.

One of, if not the most, important revelations of the paper is that tariffs do protect U.S. wages. The authors found that high school dropouts in highly protected industries, which saw tariffs quickly reduced, experienced a 17 percent lower growth in wages than high school dropouts in an industry that was not previous-ly protected.[140]

139 Ibid., 4.
140 Ibid., 14.

The national effects of NAFTA on balance seem not to have been as much of a boon as some would want you to believe, nor as much of a widespread bust as others would want you to believe. As it relates to NAFTA and, likely, most trade agreements, the results are mixed, with the negative effects based on industry, education level, and location.

In the end, what is indispu-table is that, since the passage of NAFTA, the U.S. has seen a significant increase in goods deficits with both Canada and Mexico. As we saw in Myth #8, contrary to some of the commonly advanced arguments, trade deficits are damaging. It is also important to note that, until companies share their hiring, firing, and related pay stats, we will continue to be left only with estimates of the impact of trade on employment. It is also clear that there were winners and losers, determined by education level, industry, and geography. Non-college-educated workers, industries most exposed to foreign competition, as well as the parts of the country relying on industries most exposed to foreign competition, were the most negatively impacted.

As it relates to NAFTA and, likely, most trade agreements, the results are mixed, with the negative effects based on industry, education level, and location.

16. THE U.S.-MEXICO-CANADA AGREEMENT (U.S.MCA): MORE CHANGES IN THE NAME THAN THE AGREEMENT

While the reality surrounding the new U.S.MCA is far less impressive than the rhetoric that came out of the White House, the Trump administration should be commended for trying to improve

NAFTA. Unfortunately, by the time Trump became president, there realistically wasn't much that could be done in relation to how much damage had already been done. The real lesson of the touted U.S.MCA "wins" is that they show just how much damage USA Inc.'s global trade policy has already done to the U.S. economy.

For example, one of the key "wins" of the U.S.MCA is that, by 2020, a minimum of 30 percent of the components contained in vehicles must be completed by workers earning sixteen dollars an hour. Think about that: The big wage "win" is sixteen dollars an hour. That is what we have come to—trumpeting sixteen-dollar auto manufacturing wages. Just how far have we fallen? That is $5.41, or 25 percent, less than the current national average hourly manufacturing wage of $21.41.[141] That's our big win? The U.S.MCA is more like a limbo contest: Just how low can you go? For additional perspective, consider that General Motors workers among the top tiers at an assembly plant outside of Detroit make approximately twenty-eight dollars an hour[142] while the current national average auto worker wage is twenty-two dollars an hour.[143] So why did the president agree to sixteen dollars an hour? How did we get to this point? First, lower second-tier employees at the same GM plant are

---

141 Average Hourly Earnings of Production and Non-Supervisory Employees: Manufacturing," St. Louis Federal Reserve Economic Data (FRED), Dec. 7, 2018, https://fred.stlouisfed.org/series/AHEMAN.

142 Steven Greenhouse, "New Generation of United Auto Workers Push to End Second-Tier Union Status," *The Guardian*, Sept. 13, 2015.

143 Heather Long, "Trump Says He Has a Deal With Mexico. Here's What's in It," *The Washington Post*, Aug. 27, 2018.

already down to making $17.53 an hour.[144] Additionally, according to the Center for Automotive Research, autoworkers in Mexico are making $7.34 an hour, and other sources such as Trading Economics peg the number at $2.31 an hour—that is our competition! So sixteen dollars becomes a "win." Yet some economists are decrying this as raising the cost of cars. Really? We are down to economists questioning the benefits of requiring a sixteen-dollar auto manufacturing wage? It is a sad day. How far we have fallen in our wage expectations.

Really? We are down to economists questioning the benefits of requiring a $16 auto manufacturing wage? It is a sad day. How far we have fallen in our wage expectations.

Now, some will be quick to point to automation as the real culprit of the sorry state of auto manufacturing wage trends in the U.S. They will refer to studies from highly respected professors at highly respected institutions of higher learning, stating that most job losses in manufacturing are the result of automation, not global trade. As discussed previously, how does that make seeing more manufacturing shift to Mexico anything other than adding insult to the automation injury? It's the equivalent of saying, "Don't blame NAFTA; it's automation that did the most damage. NAFTA just made it worse." Additionally, what they are leaving out is that the pressure of competing against foreign workers earning far less than American workers accelerated the process of automation. Kind of an important point.

144 Greenhouse, "New Generation."

While automation may have gotten the headlines, it was simply the manifestation or symptom of the inordinate pressure exerted on American manufacturing and wages by cheap foreign labor. Proponents of the U.S.MCA and maintaining the status quo in global trade will next tell you that, contrary to popular opinion, U.S. manufacturing is producing more than ever. Where is Paul Harvey when we need him to tell us the rest of the story? The rest of the story is that, while U.S. manufacturing output has increased, our share of global manufacturing output has not. It is, at best, misleading and, at worst, deceptive to obscure the fact that we are losing our share of global manufacturing. They will then finish by repeating glorious tales of our heightened standard of living thanks to how cheap goods are these days, noting the cheap prices of TVs and air conditioners. Last time I checked, they still fail to mention the skyrocketing costs of college, health care, and housing, items which happen to be among the largest expenses. I guess a cheap TV and air conditioner are nice to have if you are sitting at home instead of going to college or the doctor because you can barely pay your mortgage or rent. The reality is that Americans,

> What they are leaving out is that the pressure of competing against foreign workers earning far less than American workers accelerated the process of automation.

> The reality is that Americans, especially Middle America, were sold on the idea that increased foreign competition would be a windfall for them. Well, it was a windfall, just not for them.

especially Middle America, were sold on the idea that increased foreign competition would be a windfall for them. Well, it was a windfall, just not for them.

17. DOES THIS MEAN WE SHOULD STOP TRADING WITH THE REST OF THE WORLD? NO!

> *After reading this section, some may conclude that we should stop trading with the rest of the world or that I am advocating we should stop trading with the rest of the world. Let me be clear: It would be a mistake to stop trading with the rest of the world and that is not what I am advocating.*

Does all this mean we should stop trading with the rest of the world? Of course not; that's a false choice. It's an argument technique meant to stop change by falsely trying to frame new ideas as all or nothing, making them unappealing. It is meant to stop any discussion and maintain the status quo. What it does mean is that, before we blame global trade for all our economic problems or claim it is always the only answer, we need to first get better at global trade—we need to get a better return on our global trade policy. We are so bad at global trade today and so far from realizing its potential, we can't even begin to assess the merits of global trade.

Winning the game of global trade begins with awareness of these myths, as they underpin much of the current trade theory that is undermining our efforts to win in the game of global trade. It is time these myths are replaced with trade reality so that we can base trade theory and policy on reality, not myths. Only when we replace these false premises, will we be able to formulate effective global trade policy. It's time we base our trade policy on today's trade reality, not economic theory that is detached from economic reality. That is how we get a better ROI from global trade for the shareholders of USA Inc.

18. CHINA'S TRADE POLICY IS FAR SHREWDER THAN THE FORMER SOVIET UNION'S

While the former Soviet Union's government would generally only trade with its fellow Communist countries, China's government is more strategic and will trade with any country if it has the advantage.

It is instructive to compare China's and the former Soviet Union's trade policies and the varied economic impacts. The Chinese government has a brilliant trade policy. They lend us the money to buy their goods, they get the jobs associated with producing the goods we buy from them, and we get increasing welfare costs, increasing deficits, and a demoralized population. Great for China, bad for us.

> The Chinese government has a brilliant trade policy. They lend us the money to buy their goods, they get the jobs associated with producing the goods we buy from them, and we get increasing welfare costs, increasing deficits, and a demoralized population.

How brilliant is their strategy? In 2018, $382 billion brilliant. That is how much more China sold to us in goods than we did to them. In this way, the Chinese government is far more strategic than the former Soviet Union's government. The former Soviet Union would generally only trade with its fellow Communist countries. The economic impact can be seen by comparing the year-over-year increase in real GDP per capita during the last sixteen years of the Soviet Union to the growth in real GDP per capita of China over the last sixteen years. While the average rate of growth in the Soviet Union's GDP per capita was 0.3 percent from 1976 to 1991, the Chinese economy has grown, on average, 7.1 percent from 2001 through 2016.[145]

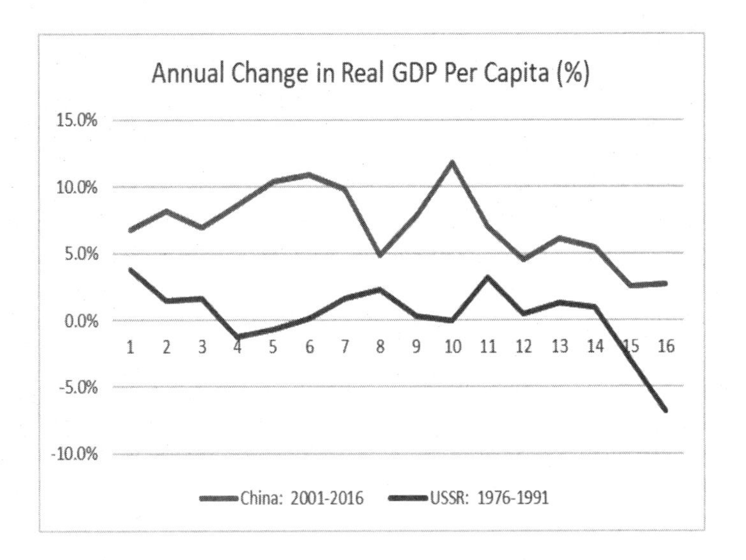

Source: Maddison Project Database

145 Jutta Bolt, Robert Inklaar, Herman de Jong, and Jan Luiten van Zanden, "Rebasing 'Maddison': New Income Comparisons and the Shape of Long-Run Economic Development," Maddison Project Database, Version 2018, Maddison Project Working Paper 10.

From 1976-1991, real GDP per capita in the former Soviet Union was essentially flat, while China's real GDP per capita increased 2.8 times from 2001 to 2016. Whereas the Soviet Union placed spreading its ideology above increasing economic growth, China viewed increasing economic growth as a means to spread its ideology. The Chinese government is far more pragmatic than the former Soviet Union. It will trade with us all day, every day, if it can get the better of us, as the Chinese are today. It's a brilliant strategy that is costing us a fortune and, among other things, leading us to fund their military buildup. Enough! You deserve better, we can do better, and it begins with both basing future trade policy on the trade realities outlined and implementing the solutions outlined. Here's to the future United States of champs, not chumps.

19. U.S.DEBT TO CHINA: MUTUALLY ASSURED FINANCIAL DESTRUCTION

If you owe a bank $100, that's your problem. If you owe a bank $100 million, that the bank's problem.

—J. Paul Getty

Next, I will address something that concerns many Americans: the massive debt we owe China. According to the U.S. Treasury Department, as of December 2018, China owns more than $1.1 trillion in U.S. debt. Some say this means China "owns" us. Why? The concern is that, if China dumps U.S. Treasurys, the value of U.S. Treasurys will plummet, increasing the rate of interest, making it costly for the U.S.to issue more debt, crippling our economy. First, if the value of Treasurys drops that much, it will be very painful for China, as it would significantly decrease the value of assets China owns—its more than $1 trillion in U.S. Treasurys. Second, if interest rates spike, we won't be able to borrow from China to buy their goods, which would be a massive problem for China. Remember the state-owned enterprises that employ millions of Chinese workers? If we stopped buying China's goods, they would be decimated, leaving many Chinese people without jobs—a recipe for political unrest.

> If we stopped buying China's goods, they would be decimated, leaving many Chinese people without jobs—a recipe for political unrest.

Still, others are concerned that we owe so much we won't be able to pay China back. News flash... China's government doesn't want us to pay them back. In what else could they invest more than $1 trillion with the same low level of risk? Additionally, we are like the credit card borrower who carries a massive balance and never misses a payment—we are a lender's dream. This puts the U.S. and China in an interesting financial situation: If China dumps U.S. Treasurys, it also suffers and conversely, if we default, we suffer. We are, to a large degree, stuck with and financially dependent on each other: We need their loans to buy their goods and they need us to buy their goods because they produce things, while we produce welfare checks.

20. TALK VS. TARIFFS: U.S.-CHINA TRADE

"The right approach is for all to sit down as equals to find solutions."

—Chinese Premier Li Keqiang

I will finish this section with the ongoing trade competition between the U.S. and China. First, China and the U.S. will always be in a trade competition—maybe not a war, but ongoing angling to gain an advantage in the trade relationship. Even if President Trump and China announce new terms of our trading relationship, China will always be trying to gain an advantage and, hopefully, the U.S. will be too.

Some are hesitant to use tariffs to push China for trade concessions. They point out that China could retaliate against increased U.S. tariffs on Chinese goods in many ways. First, it can slow the flow of USA Inc.'s goods entering China, and it has. This can be indirectly through increased inspections of U.S. goods, which was reported by Reuters sources as having already occurred.[146] Regulations could also be used to limit or prevent USA Inc.'s goods from entering China. China has also flat-out stopped the entry of some USA Inc.'s goods. A preliminary injunction was placed by a Chinese court on sales of goods by the American company Micron Technology.[147] China even has options to retaliate against U.S. companies operating in China. While these companies are insulated from Chinese tariffs on imported U.S. goods, their operations require people, and China could restrict visas for the employees they need. China could also devalue its currency, but this has risks, as a weakened currency can create financial imbalances, sowing the seeds of a financial crisis. Chinese consumers could be prodded into boycotting American goods using state-owned media to whip

146 Ryan Woo, "What Can Beijing Do if China-U.S. Trade Row Worsens?" Reuters, June 19, 2018

147 Richard Waters, "Trump Tariffs Trigger Anxiety for U.S. Chipmakers," *Financial Times*, July 5, 2018.

up anti-American sentiment. A byproduct of this could be reduced tourism to the U.S. While these are all possible, China's economy is already slowing, placing pressure on its ability to provide jobs for its citizens. They will also be sensitive to doing anything that weakens U.S. companies operating in China and employing Chinese citizens. China also understands that a sudden and significant reduction in U.S. purchases of Chinese goods would be devastating for its economy.

At some point, enough white-collar workers will also be impacted, and that is when the real, seismic political change will occur.

At some point, China may realize on its own that the current U.S.-China trade imbalance is unsustainable and will agree to modifications which allow the U.S.to move toward a more sustainable trading relationship with China. Alternatively, one day, maybe sooner than expected, China will have this realization forced upon itself through a financially painful event that would be far more damaging than gradual, measured modifications to the current U.S.-China trading relationship. The U.S. cannot endlessly borrow money from China to buy the goods that are putting American workers out of jobs and exerting downward pressure on American wages. Why not? Because at some point, enough white-collar workers would also be impacted, and that is when the real, seismic political change would occur.

If you think Trump's actions on trade were drastic, wait until enough of the electorate is severely impacted by our trade policy. Rather than wait until that political upheaval, it would be wise for both China and the U.S.to undertake measures that equalize their trading relationship. Remember, it is economic desperation that provides the most fertile ground for extremist ideas. Let's just hope China realizes that too.

Remember, it is economic desperation that provides the most fertile ground for extremist ideas.

SECTION III

REDUCING FINANCIAL CRISES: A THRIVING MAIN STREET REQUIRES A STABLE WALL STREET

We have an OPM: Other People's Money financial system. The money that banks use to make loans is not their own. This, along with loan quantity over quality compensation systems, creates an unstable source of consumer and company loans, the lifeblood of a growing economy.

21. LOANS ARE THE LIFEBLOOD OF A GROWING ECONOMY

Loans are the lifeblood of a growing economy. Just as all living things wither without water, Main Street withers when our banking system is in financial crisis. The economy depends on credit cards, automobile loans, home loans, and loans to companies. When credit is available, consumers spend more, while companies can expand at a greater rate. This is especially important to small business owners, as they are more dependent on financing than larger companies having billions of dollars in cash on their balance sheets.

Just as all living things wither without water, Main Street withers when our banking system is in financial crisis.

Maybe most importantly, it is not just loan availability that is critical to our economy, but consumer and business confidence in the stability of our financial system. Why is that so critical? Even when loans are available, if consumers and businesses are unsure about the future availability of financing, they will limit borrowing and hold excess cash in reserve for times when financing isn't available. That stunts consumer spending and business investment, key drivers of economic growth.

22. MOVING BEYOND FINANCIAL FEAST AND FAMINE

Due to the seminal importance of financing to our economy, the solutions in this section are designed to create a more consistent source of consumer and company loans. This is done by focusing on reducing the frequency and severity of financial crises. Moderating the damaging swings from excessive capital availability to capital scarcity would also increase bank lending capacity when loans are needed most, during periods of economic slowing. The solutions would

If consumers and businesses are unsure about the future availability of financing, they will limit borrowing and hold excess cash in reserve for times when financing isn't available.

moderate the magnitude of economic downturns, lessening the pain inflicted on consumers and small business owners. It would also reduce the likelihood for future taxpayer-funded bailouts. The solutions would provide a highly desirable return on investment for consumers and small business owners as well as American taxpayers who are on the hook for bank bailouts.

The solutions would provide a highly desirable return on investment for consumers and small business owners as well as American taxpayers who are on the hook for bank bailouts.

The Flawed Argument for Maintaining a System That Favors Taxpayer Bailouts

Some may argue that the solutions would reduce the quantity of loans available. First, this argument judges the solutions based solely on their potential impact on loan availability during periods of *peak* economic growth. It ignores the rest of the economic cycle, including the periods when loans are most needed: when growth is slowing. The solutions in this section are focused on ensuring loans are consistently available, especially during periods of economic slowing, when they are needed most, not how much financing is available during boom times.

Second, how much financing was available in 2009? How about 2010? Not much. The solutions are designed to increase loan availability by reducing the frequency and severity of periods like 2009. Ask yourself this: Would reducing subprime mortgage loans in 2007 have been a problem or would it have helped? Were we better off focusing on maximizing loans during 2007, as opposed to ensuring the financial system would still be able to provide loans in 2009? Loans are scarce during recessions partially because a) financial institutions lend the most money when asset valuations are the highest and competition for loans is the greatest, b) the heightened competition forces them to make loans on very aggressive terms, making the loans riskier, c) asset valuations and economic growth eventually decline, and d) this leads to increased loan default rates, leaving banks with less money to lend when the economy needs it most. It is as certain as death and taxes, at least under today's compensation systems that encourage bank executives and those approving loans to make as many loans as possible. More on the pivotal role compensation systems play in financial crises later.

> The solutions in this section are focused on ensuring loans are consistently available, especially during periods of economic slowing, when they are needed most.

Based on the devastating effects on our financial system, economy, and home prices, prioritizing having as many mortgage loans available as possible in 2007 did not turn out well for the shareholders of USA Inc. According to the St. Louis Federal Reserve, subsequent to the Great Financial Crisis, Americans experienced a loss of 8.7 million jobs and a massive decline in asset values across many classes. Worrying about a moderation in loan availability during periods when there is already ample capital is the equivalent of a bar owner worrying he or she won't be able to overserve patrons. It may be profitable for the bar owner to overserve customers and feel good to the patrons in the short term, but it leads to bad decisions and a hangover. Similarly, increasing lending when capital is already freely flowing can lead to bad decisions and one heck of an economic hangover to the point of requiring bailouts by the American taxpayer.

> Pumping more and more loans into the financial system when the economy is growing rapidly is like taking antibiotics when you are feeling well—you not only don't need them, but you won't have them when you are ill.

> The solutions are focused on ensuring consistent financing is available throughout an economic cycle, not a system that prioritizes and promotes financing during boom times.

The question isn't how much financing is available during boom times; rather, how to ensure consistent financing is available during all times, especially during periods of slowing economic growth. When the economy is growing rapidly and financing is flowing freely, increasing loan availability even further is like taking antibiotics when you are feeling well—you not only don't need them, but you won't have them when you are ill. The solutions are focused on ensuring consistent financing is available throughout an economic cycle, not a system that prioritizes and promotes financing during boom times.

It is the difference between a system that prioritizes pumping more and more loans into the financial system even when asset prices are elevated and loan quality is reduced, and implementing a system that prioritizes maintaining a consistent flow of consumer and company loans.

Even Adam Smith Knew This Would Be a Problem

Some may say the solutions proposed in this section aren't necessary because the "market" will monitor itself. They may view banks as being capable of unilaterally reducing financial crises and ensuring a steadier supply of consumer and company loans.

First, even Adam Smith knew that human nature was such that excessive borrowing and lending would occur during boom times: "When the profits of trade happen to be greater than ordinary, over-trading becomes a general error...,"[148] which is another way of saying during boom periods.

Second, the "market" as a self-regulator only works when market participants have incentives to self-regulate. Conversely, when the bank executives and loan officers comprising the "market" have incentives to approve more and more loans, the idea of solely relying on the "market" to prevent financial crises is, at best, overly optimistic. Compensation systems based on loan quantity aren't set up to increase stability; they are set up to increase lending activity. This is especially dangerous when asset values are elevated and hyper-competition due to excessive liquidity requires making loans on increasingly risky terms to maintain market share. The proposed solutions would give the theory of the "market" acting as a self-regulator the opportunity to become a reality.

> The solutions proposed give the theory of the "market" acting as a self-regulator the opportunity to become a reality.

Third, the damaging effects of loan-quantity compensation systems

148 Adam Smith, *The Wealth of Nations,* Volume I, Book IV, 459.

are exacerbated by the FDIC's explicit guarantee of customer deposits and the federal government's implicit promise to bail out banks. Collectively, these create a recipe for excessive risk-taking, not self-moderation.

Fourth, as we will see, banks make loans using other people's money. This further reduces their financial incentive to manage the financial system in a way that reduces banking boom and bust cycles.

Creating a more stable financial system begins with understanding how our financial system works.

Get the Money Back!

What makes a financial system stable? As simple as it sounds, getting the money back.

What makes a financial system stable? As simple as it sounds, getting the money back.

When I worked at the finance arm of General Electric, GE Commercial Finance, the number one truism was a very simple but powerful one: We make money by getting our money back. Similarly, a stable financial system depends on loans being paid back. Otherwise, banks will no longer have money to lend. Like most things in life, however, sometimes the most obvious and important things, like getting the money back, are not the sole priority. To understand why, we first have to understand how our financial system works.

23. WE HAVE AN OPM BANKING SYSTEM

Wall Street's Main Street Impact

We have an OPM: Other People's Money financial system. This includes money banks and other lending institutions get from Wall Street. The availability of bank loans depends partially on the activities and stability of Wall Street. First, Wall Street helps banks borrow money, which they then lend to consumers and businesses. Wall Street also helps make loans available through asset-backed loans. These are loans backed, or secured by assets such as automobiles, all types of equipment, and other assets. When Wall Street isn't working properly, loan availability decreases. When loans aren't available, consumers and businesses borrow less, which means consumers buy less and businesses invest less. How important is this? During the financial crisis of 2008, asset-backed financing, the lifeblood of many auto loans, dried up. According to the St. Louis Federal Reserve, vehicle sales plummeted by almost half, falling from an annual rate of 17.22 million vehicles in February of 2007 to 9.22 million vehicles a year in February of 2009. This drastic decline in vehicle sales pushed automobile manufacturers to the brink of bankruptcy, putting millions of jobs at risk. This is just one example of how critical a stable flow of financing is to our economy.

Banks Depend on You

Banks also use your money—a lot of your money—to make loans. The vast majority of the money banks have and use to lend comes from the savings that depositors like you keep at banks in the form of savings accounts, money market accounts, and certificates of deposit. It also comes from you if you are a small business owner when you deposit your company's earnings at your bank. Large businesses also supply the money banks lend using the profits they deposit at their banks, profits you generate through your purchases. How much are we talking about? As of the third quarter of 2018, $13.5 trillion[149] of your money. As a result, and this is critically important, banks are making loans using other people's money, not their money. This use of other people's money can create what is called the principal-agent problem.

Banking's Principal-Agent Problem

The principal-agent problem is when you (the principal) and the person you rely on to represent and protect your interests (the agent) have differing interests. When this happens, there is the possibility for the agent to act in a way that benefits them at the expense of the principal they are supposed to be representing.

In our banking system, the principals are you and me, while the agents are the banks. This is a necessary system, as most people don't have the time or expertise to make loans, and even if they did, most individuals don't have enough money to provide the loans consumers and corporations need to keep our economy going. The problem occurs when the principal-agent problem in our banking

149 FDIC Quarterly, Quarterly Banking Profile: Third Quarter 2018", Table II-A and NCUA, in "Quarterly Credit Union Summary 2018 Q3", Federal Deposit Insurance Corporation, Summary of Federally Insured Credit Union Call Report Data, 4.

system isn't accounted for and even exacerbated, as they are in our current financial system.

> The problem occurs when the principal-agent problem in our banking system isn't accounted for and even exacerbated, as they are in our current financial system.

Loan-Quantity-Based Compensation Systems

Bank executive compensation is directly or indirectly tied to how many loans are made. It is a system of compensation that rewards loan quantity: Bank executives get paid more when they make more loans. There is even a phrase for this priority of making loans: "Get the money out the door." Just as car dealers are focused on getting cars out the door, financial institutions are focused on getting the money out the door. As a result, our banking system is based on making more and more loans. Don't get me wrong—banks want to get the money they lend back. The reality is also that, if the bank executives and individuals making loan approval decisions are paid based on how many loans they make and not at least as much based on how many of the loans are paid back, loan *quantity* trumps loan *quality*. Consider the metaphor used by the former CEO of Citigroup, Charles Prince, in 2007 leading up to the subprime financial crisis to describe the need to continue making loans to keep up with competitors: "As long as the music is playing, you've got to get up and dance."[150] This is a problem when a stable financial system requires getting

150 Maria Aspan, "Ex-Citi CEO Defends 'Dancing' Quote to U.S. Panel," Reuters, April 8, 2010

the money back. The degree to which banks prioritize loan quantity over quality varies from bank to bank and changes depending on what point in the economic cycle they are in. One bank may decline several loans, while another approves them because they are prioritizing increasing their market share.

When the individuals making loan approval decisions are paid based on how many loans they make and not at least as much based on how many of the loans they make are paid back, loan *quantity* trumps loan *quality*.

It is like giving someone money to go to Las Vegas to bet on your behalf and saying, "The more you bet, the more I will pay *regardless* the results," and, "Don't worry, it's my money you are betting, not yours, so just make sure you bet it all." It encourages risky behavior, behavior that creates an unstable financial system. It should be obvious that, if the people approving loans are paid, first and foremost, based on how many loans they approve, you are eventually going to have a problem.

If those approving loans are paid based more on the *quantity* of loans they approve than the *quality* of the loans, then you have a recipe for financial crises.

Banks Don't Make Loans, People Do

Some have argued for requiring lending institutions to put more skin in the game. This means banks keeping more of the loans they make on their balance sheet (maintaining ownership of the loans), as opposed to selling them to investors. Seems logical. Wouldn't banks be more selective if they stood to lose more money when loans go bad? While that is an improvement, the flaw in this solution is the following: Banks don't approve loans, people do. Bank employees decide whether a loan is approved. If the individuals approving loans are still paid on loan volume, they will continue making more loans—follow the money, not the regulations.

> It should be obvious that if the people approving loans are paid first and foremost based on how many loans they approve, you are eventually going to have a problem.

Why not just increase bank regulations? Again, even if you further regulate the legal entities known as banks, if the individuals approving loans are still paid based on loan volume, making more loans will remain a priority. There is a solution, and rather than adding more regulations, it has to do with bank executive compensation. But what may surprise some is that it doesn't require limiting bank employee pay.

> Follow the money, not the regulations.

Compensating for Wall Street's Principal-Agent Problem

Some argue for limiting the compensation of bankers. While this is popular and appeals to the anger Main Street feels over the damage caused by the collapse of our financial system, this too would fail. Why? The problem isn't how much bankers are paid;

The problem isn't how much bankers are paid; it is when bankers are paid predominantly based on how much money they lend.

the problem is when bankers are paid predominantly based on how much money they lend. Bank instability increases when bank compensation is disproportionately tied to loan quantity. Until this is changed, our financial system will continue to experience episodes of significant loan defaults, reduced loan availability, and the lingering effects of uncertainty which holds back consumer and business borrowing.

If the goal is to ensure a stable flow of consumer and corporate loans and that requires loans being paid back, then bank executive compensation should be at least equally tied to whether the loans are paid back.

Borrowing the Profit: Dividend Recapitalizations

When compensation systems reward loan quantity over quality this can lead to loans that anyone outside of the financial industry wouldn't imagine were even possible. This occurs when an excessive amount of loans are available and the pressure to maintain bank market share is at its peak. When this occurs, borrowers buying another company can sometimes get loans that include not only the money needed to buy the company, but also to pay themselves a dividend at closing. This allows the acquiring company to make a substantial profit the first day they own the company. How? It is called a dividend recapitalization. This is a fancy term for getting the bank to lend you the money to pay yourself a profit up front, before you even do anything.

It is a sweet deal. How many of these loans have been made? According to *The Wall Street Journal,* at one point during the frenetic peak of the previous cycle, $73.2 billion of dividend recapitalization loans were made in 2007.[151] To put this in perspective, according to Reuters, during the period between July 1 and August 6, 2015, $8.3 billion of these loans were announced. Why would a bank lend money to companies in the business of acquiring other companies to pay themselves a profit rather than to use the borrowed money to expand, invest in research and development, or buy another company? This is what happens when loan quantity trumps loan quality.

> This is a fancy term for getting the bank to lend you the money to pay yourself a profit up front, before you even do anything.

It's Not Just a Bank Problem

The incentive problem isn't isolated to traditional FDIC-insured banks. Automobile finance companies have an incentive problem, but with a twist. Most of the major automakers have what are called captive finance arms. These are finance companies owned by the automobile manufacturers. They loan money to people like you and me to buy a car and sell the loans and loan repayment obligations to Wall Street. Wall Street bundles them into what are called asset-backed loans and sells them to investors.

151 Jennifer Rossa, "The Ghost of Dividend Recaps Past," *The Wall Street Journal*, Aug. 21, 2009, http://blogs.wsj.com/privateequity/2009/08/21/the-ghost-of-dividend-recaps-past/.

Why do they do this? First, because, when times are good, the loans are profitable. Second, it enables automotive manufacturers to sell more cars than they would if the financing weren't available. Don't have the money to buy a car? That's okay, they will loan you the money...including to individuals with weaker credit. All so they can sell more cars. For years, companies have used financing to sell more. I bought a very old GE refrigerator salesman manual that discusses financing provided by GE to buyers of their refrigerators. This (along with the job losses) is why, when asset-backed financing dried up during the financial crisis, automobile sales plummeted. And it is occurring again. Subprime loans aren't restricted to home mortgages. More than 21 percent of auto loan originations are subprime.[152]

If compensation were tied to loan performance, bank employees could be paid more, and shareholders of USA Inc. would still come out ahead. Why? Because the likelihood of repeating the 2008 financial crisis and its long-term economic costs would be reduced.

<u>Financial Crises Solution #1</u>: Base non-salary compensation of executives and those approving loans at federally insured financial institutions and systemically important financial institutions, as designated under the Dodd-Frank Act "SIFI," on how much of the money they lend is repaid. This would ensure that our primary interest, them getting our money back and ensuring a stable source of loans, is also their primary interest.

152 Jonathan Schwarzberg, "Rush of Dividend Loans for U.S.Private Equity Firms," Reuters, Aug. 6, 2015.

Instant Lender Gratification and "Get the Money Out the Door Faster!"

Tying compensation to loan performance is a critical first step, but another problem remains. Currently, those approving loans get paid when the loans are *made*, not when they are *repaid*. Back to our gambling analogy—we not only tell our gambler that he will get paid whether he wins, but we pay him at the beginning of each hand rather than at the end. He doesn't even have to see how his bet did!

There are two types of loans that reveal the gravity of this flaw in the banking compensation systems. The first is an I/O, or interest-only loan. With this type of loan, the borrower pays back none of the money borrowed, also known as principal during the I/O period term, instead paying only the interest owed. This is in contrast to what is called an amortizing loan, in which the borrower's payments include not only the interest owed, but repayment of the principal. An example would be if you borrowed money to buy a house and only had to make the interest payments, not repaying any of the money borrowed during the life of the loan. These were part of the fabric of the subprime mortgage crisis. Importantly, while the principal of the loan isn't repaid during the I/O period, the bank is getting paid its profit, known as interest. Banks get their profit immediately, while our principal remains at risk—that only exacerbates the principal-agent problem.

Banks get their profit immediately, while our principal remains at risk—that only exacerbates the principal-agent problem.

A second type of loan, a payment-in-kind or PIK loan,

takes the concept of delaying principal repayment to a whole new level. The borrower not only doesn't repay any of the principal during the I/O period, but amazingly, borrows more money from the lender to pay the interest payments on the loan. The lender actually lends them more of our money to pay the interest, also known as the bank's profit. The bank uses our money to pay themselves a profit before our money is repaid. Welcome to the alternative universe known as our financial system.

The bank uses our money to pay themselves a profit before our money is repaid. Welcome to the alternative universe known as our financial system.

At this point, you might be asking, "Why in the world would banks do this?" It's simple: If they don't, they will make fewer loans, losing market share to their competitors making less money. How real is this drive to maintain market share? Remember the colorful metaphor used by Prince in 2007 leading up to the subprime financial crisis to describe the need to keep up with competitors: "As long as the music is playing, you've got to get up and dance."[153] And remember, how do bank executives make more money? That's right, by making more loans. How do you make more loans? Make it easier for companies to borrow by reducing the amount they have to pay back during the life of the loan. As we saw, sometimes they even lend them the money to pay the interest on the loan.

After reading this, some may argue for preventing these types of loans. There is a different solution.

153 Aspan, "Ex-Citi CEO."

Financial Crises Solution #2: Pay the non-salary compensation of executives and those approving loans at federally insured financial institutions and SIFIs as they get our money back, not up front. The slower the loans get paid back, the slower they get paid. This would make our interest, getting our money back in a timely manner, the banks' interest. While banks could still make I/O and PIK loans, there would be less of an incentive to make them, because they wouldn't get fully paid until the loans were repaid, replacing instant gratification with ROI-based compensation.

Compensation systems in which bank executives and loan officers are paid to make endless loans leads lenders to chase market share over loan quality and increases the likelihood of future loan losses. Those losses reduce the ability of banks to lend, creating recessions, leaving companies and consumers without the loans they desperately need during recessions. A key question should be whether the policy under consideration will increase the availability of loans when we most need them: during periods of economic slowing. That is how the American taxpayer will avoid future bailouts and get a better return on the financial guarantee it provides to the financial system.

A key question should be whether the policy under consideration will increase the availability of loans when we most need them: during periods of economic slowing.

More than Just a Cost of Doing Business

Tying the compensation of individuals working at lending institutions to loan performance and paying bank executives as loans are repaid are the first steps necessary to stabilize our financial system. But that's not enough.

You may have heard of the billions in financial penalties some banks paid relating to subprime mortgage loans. Even after billions were paid in penalties, the institutions paying the settlements still generated billions in profits while the executives made millions. Additionally, when some of the largest financial institutions were on the brink of failure, they were bailed out. If you were an executive that made millions and your bank was bailed out, what incentive would you have to not do the same thing again? None. While some financial institutions were allowed to fail, the largest, most important federally insured banks were not. They had no risk of ruin. Risk of ruin is just as it sounds, the risk of losing everything *and* being unable to continue. With no risk of ruin, there is no incentive to change behavior, especially when there is the potential for billions of dollars of profits and millions of dollars of compensation.

If you know the penalty will be less than the profits, you will personally make millions, and risk of ruin isn't a certainty, you have every incentive to engage in the same risky behavior.

If you know the penalty will be less than the profits, you will personally make millions, and risk of ruin isn't a certainty, you have every incentive to engage in the same risky behavior.

This creates a moral hazard, which is when the potential negative consequences associated with a risky behavior are removed, encouraging the behavior. Without a change in compensation systems, there will be no incentive to change and every incentive to repeat the same personally enriching behavior. Then we will, again, be talking about lending institutions being on the brink of failure and debating whether to bail them out. Yet incredibly, someone will once again say, "We couldn't have seen this coming."

Some have argued the answer is to simply not bail out failing financial institutions. However, while maybe emotionally appealing, that is not practical. A working financial system is critical to economic and job growth. Allowing financial institutions to fail on a wholesale level would cripple the economy, devastating the lives of many Americans. However, there are other solutions to reduce the moral hazard.

What Regulators Can Learn from College Athletics

There is a series of solutions that would go a long way in reducing the moral hazard currently found in our financial system, solutions which take a page from how college athletics deals with rules infractions.

When an infraction in college athletics is severe enough, the university may be required to vacate its victories. In the world of business, profits are the equivalent of victories. Only when the penalties for financial institution infractions are severe enough that the penalties are greater than the profits will financial institution behavior change. The key is for the financial penalties to create a significant deterrence, not a financial slap on the wrist. Today, it remains more profitable to engage in the non-sanctioned behavior, even if caught. The penalty must be materially greater than the financial benefit received from the risky behavior. It must be severe enough to change behavior.

> Only when the penalties for financial institution infractions are severe enough that the penalties are greater than the profits will financial institution behavior change.

Financial Crises Solution #3: Penalties are in an amount equal to all the profits earned from the behavior plus 20 percent, ensuring that the profit from taking the risk is eliminated and critically, that there is a deterrent. These funds will be placed into a system-wide bailout fund.

Also, as in college athletics, when infractions are serious enough, the coach may be removed. This leads to our next solution.

Financial Crises Solution #4: Remove executives from federally insured financial institutions and SIFIs cited for infractions, and bar them from working in the financial services industry or as lobbyists, for a period of ten years. Require that an amount equal to all the compensation paid to the executive during the last five years, and compensation owed in the future, be paid by the lending institution into the same bailout fund previously mentioned.

Rather than limiting bank compensation, let the banks decide if they are going to risk paying twice: once to the executives and then again to the bailout fund. Then they might consider basing their compensation systems more on loan quality.

Some might voice concerns that implementing these compensation-related solutions would lead to the loss of the current captains of our financial industry, their lieutenants, and their expertise. What expertise would that be? The expertise of the chief executives of the largest financial institutions hauled before Congress, whose common refrain was that they couldn't have seen the financial crisis coming?

Returning to what we can learn from college athletics, consider what happens when the athletic program's infractions are extremely serious. In this case, the program may be shut down. This leads to our next solution, the equivalent of what is referred to as the "death penalty" in college athletics.

Financial Crises Solution #5: If a federally insured financial institution or SIFI requires additional capital to continue operations, the shareholders don't provide the additional capital, no other private source of capital is obtained, and a bailout is deemed necessary to avoid a financial crisis, ownership of the lending institution goes to the taxpayers and all its shareholders are wiped out.

If the taxpayers are going to bail out the bank, they should reap future benefits if the bank returns to profitability. The bank would be sold to investors once it is profitable again, and would not remain a taxpayer-owned entity.

Penalties must be serious enough to create a real deterrent.

Making Financial Institution Self-Policing Real: Financial Jujitsu

Prevention remains the best policy. This leads to our next solution: Real self-policing. How can we get financial institutions to police themselves? Make the behavior of each financial institution relevant to the other. The following solution will provide an incentive for lending institutions to truly police

Financial Crises Wall Street Solution #6: If the previously mentioned bailout fund does not have enough money to bail out troubled institutions, require the other federally insured institutions and SIFIs to provide the necessary funding. The amount contributed by institutions to the bailout would be based on the percentage each institution's assets represent as a percent of the total federally insured financial assets in our financial system.

If, for example, a federally insured bank holds 1 percent of the total assets held by federally insured financial institutions and SIFIs, and another institution requires a $1 billion bailout, then the bank would pay 1 percent of the total bailout required, or $10 million. This would eliminate the need for a taxpayer bailout, a long-overdue accomplishment. Maybe more importantly, it would also provide a real incentive for lending institutions to truly be self-policing, which would help reduce the occurrence of the need for bailouts, the ideal scenario. If financial institutions were liable for funding the full bailout of their peers, they would likely recommend regulations that would reduce the risk of individual bailouts and a system-wide failure in the banking system. They might even lobby for them. These recommendations would be invaluable because the best source of regulations to prevent the need for bank bailouts and a system-wide failure is the lending institutions themselves, when given the necessary incentives.

If financial institutions were liable for funding the full bailout of their peers, they would likely recommend regulations that would reduce the risk of individual bailouts and a system-wide failure in the banking system. They might even lobby for them.

This solution would leverage both the lobbying power of the largest financial institutions and turn the size of the largest banks into an ally, a sort of financial jujitsu. For example, according to SNL Financial, the five largest banks hold 44 percent of the banking industries' assets. If these five financial institutions were liable for nearly 50 percent of future bailouts, certainly they would want some restrictions on their peers' lending activities.

Regulators Flying Blind

Where were the regulators during the period leading up to and including the 2008 financial crisis? Most may assume that regulators including the Federal Reserve had unlimited power to demand information from financial institutions. It would have been reasonable to assume that regulators had more than enough information to know what risks banks were taking. However, through my interactions with the Federal Reserve, I learned this was not true.

My awakening to the limitations placed on the Federal Reserve's ability to get information from the very financial institutions they regulate began with one simple but shocking phone call. During a phone call with the Federal Reserve, I asked what type of financial information they would like to have for a new center of excellence they were considering setting up. I had expected a long list of very sophisticated financial information. To my surprise and shock, the list included rudimentary items, items that I assumed they would have already had, and importantly, needed in their role as regulators and in oversight of federally insured banks. After I recovered from my dismay, when I asked why they didn't already have the information, the reply was, "The Paperwork Reduction Act of 1999." It was explained to me that, to obtain information beyond what was currently being received, the Federal Reserve needed to submit a request to the Office of Management and Budget, also known as the OMB. The OMB would then ask the financial institutions how much it would cost them to produce the information. If the OMB deemed the cost to be too much, the information request was denied. While it is absurd that the Federal Reserve can't obtain the information needed to properly oversee the banks and ensure the stability of the financial system we all depend on, a greater concern is the following: If providing the information requested by the Federal Reserve was truly cost-prohibitive to the financial institution, it means the financial institution didn't have the information. This is concerning, to say the least. This leads to our next solution.

Financial Crises Solution #7: Permit the Federal Reserve to obtain the information it requests, so long as the information is not already being sent to another regulator.

If providing the information requested by the Federal Reserve was truly cost-prohibitive to the financial institution, it means the financial institution didn't have the information. This is concerning, to say the least.

Some may object to the potential increased costs to banks. They may argue that it would push up the cost of lending and reduce the availability of capital. While this is a typical fallback argument in response to a request for additional information, it rings hollow when examined. First, well-run financial institutions should already have the information being requested so it shouldn't be a massive cost burden. Second, even if there were additional costs, the costs would be an insignificant price to pay compared to the jobs lost in the economy and wealth destroyed in the stock markets when the financial system froze up as it did in 2008.

24. OVERCOMING OBSTACLES TO IMPLEMENTING FINANCIAL SYSTEM SOLUTIONS BEGINS WITH CONGRESS

Do You Even Know or Care How to Spell Finance?

At the end of my meeting with the chief of staff of the U.S. Senate Committee on Finance after the last financial crisis, he said that Secretary of the Treasury Timothy Geithner would be testifying before the committee the next day. He wanted to know: if I could ask the secretary one question, what would I ask? I didn't think much of the request until the next day when I attended Geithner's hearing. Then I understood why he asked me that question.

The Senate committee hearing began and one by one, each senator asked their initial question of Geithner. The questions seemed well thought out and related to the financial system. However, the same could not be said of the second round of questions, which were clearly not as well-scripted and seemed to come out of left field. At that point, not only was it painfully obvious that each senator was ill-prepared and not well versed in our financial system, they didn't have enough questions to go around. The combination of lack of preparation and limited knowledge of finance on the part of some was stunning, given that our financial system had just experienced the most significant financial crisis since the Great Depression. It was a crisis which, as I will discuss later, had been only days away from turning into a complete financial meltdown. It

> *It seemed likely…the senators had spent more time the evening before at campaign fundraisers than preparing for Secretary Geithner's testimony.*

seemed likely, based on that second round of questions, that the senators had spent more time the evening before at campaign fundraisers than preparing for Geithner's testimony.

After the hearing, I understood why I was asked what question I would ask—they needed questions to feed to the senators. It seems that there is limited expertise to lose in the Senate if the limits on tenure I discuss later were applied to finance-related committees. The senators' questions also inspired the following solution:

Financial Crises Solution #8: Require members of Congress serving on finance-related committees or subcommittees to complete a minimum number of continuing education hours on how our financial system works, along with specialized seminars relating to the various sectors of our financial system. For example, members who serve on the House Subcommittee on Housing and Insurance would attend seminars on the housing industry and insurance industry, while members of the House Subcommittee on Monetary Policy and Trade would be required to earn a minimum number of continuing education hours related to monetary policy and trade. These would not be taught by lobbyists or banks, rather by academics.

This would not only lead to more knowledgeable committee members, but also broader knowledge within the entire Congress as finance committee tenure limits would allow more members to serve on finance committees. This is important because all members vote on bills, not just committee members. Maybe most important, it would further one of the goals discussed in Section V, Increasing Congressional Transparency and Accountability, making being a member of Congress less cushy. Members would have to spend time learning about at least one subject they influence, a subject which impacts each of us daily, even if it cuts into their time spent fundraising.

How do we get Congress to implement these solutions? While this is discussed in Section V, Increasing Congressional Transparency and Accountability, below is a brief preview, including three solutions that will be especially important if we are going to have a chance to implement the solutions in this section.

First, it is much more difficult to exert influence when you don't know who to influence. This leads to our first two campaign-donation-related solutions.

Congressional Solution #22: Randomly assign committee chairmanships and committee assignments.

The potential objections that this would deprive the shareholders of USA Inc. of the expertise built up by members serving on the same finance committees for years has even less credence, given the Great Financial Crisis. If anything, I'd like to see new members as opposed to the same members who were on the committees overseeing our financial system when the last financial crisis occurred.

Congressional Solution #23: Require campaign donations to be made before committee chairmanships and assignments are determined.

By requiring donations be made before committee assignments are determined, this eliminates the ability of donors to give large sums of cash to the election campaigns of those serving on committees impacting the donors' industries and businesses. If you don't know who the chairman or members of the congressional committees impacting your industry or business will be, you won't know who to give the bags of money to.

> If you don't know who the chairman or members of the congressional committees impacting your industry or business will be, you won't know who to give the bags of money to.

Wealthy donors, especially a problem in the financial industry, might just give to all members of Congress and their PACs to ensure their bases are covered, but there is a solution for that too:

Congressional Solution #24: If donors give money to members of Congress who are subsequently assigned to committees that impact the donor's industry or business, the member must return the money to the donor.

These solutions would reduce the power of and vulnerability of financial committee members to the influence of outsized political campaign contributions. While some may point out that given the recent rulings of our Supreme Court, these measures might not survive judicial review even if implemented, that doesn't mean we shouldn't pursue the solutions. It means we need to pursue them, implement them, and, if they are struck down, devise alternative solutions until we find the solutions that achieve the objective and withstand legal challenges. The answer isn't giving up; the answer is creativity and commitment to achieving the objective.

25. WERE BANK BAILOUTS NECESSARY?

Let me finish with a hotly contested question as it relates to the 2008 financial crisis: Just how close were we to a financial meltdown? Or, said another way, did we really need to bail out the financial institutions? Here, I draw on my firsthand experience working at what was, at the time, called GE Commercial Finance.

GE on the Brink: My Front Row Seat to the Financial Crisis

The week of September 15, 2008, I was working for GE Commercial Finance. I was at my desk when word spread around the company that the most secure borrower in the world, GE, could not get anyone to lend it money for twenty-four hours, a form of short-term debt known as commercial paper. This is what former Treasury Secretary Hank Paulson was referring to in his book, *On the Brink: Inside the Race to Stop the Collapse of the Global Financial System*, when he wrote that GE CEO Jeffrey Immelt confided in him that he had serious concerns about GE's ability to access the credit markets.

GE, like many companies, relied heavily on commercial paper, a very short-term form of financing. Short-term financing is generally considered among the lowest-risk type of financing, as the lender is repaid quickly. Yet the financial crisis was so serious that no institution would make even this type of twenty-four-hour loan to the most creditworthy company in the world at the time: GE. When the most creditworthy company in the world is not able to get a bank to lend it money for twenty-four hours, you know the financial system is on the brink of collapse.

The financial system had locked up, and like an engine seizing up when it runs out of oil, the financial system was on the brink of blowing up. The financial system was in desperate and immediate need of "oil."

When the most creditworthy company in the world at the time is not able to get a bank to lend it money for twenty-four hours, you know the financial system is on the brink of collapse.

As a result, on September 20, 2008, Paulson announced a

plan for massive government support of the financial system. He sought authorization from Congress to inject hundreds of billions of dollars, the oil which our financial system was in such desperate need of, into the financial system. Some on Capitol Hill protested that they were being asked to authorize hundreds of billions of dollars in bailout funds yet had only a three-page memo outlining the terms. They didn't get it. They didn't understand the gravity of the situation and, more importantly, they didn't understand that the purpose of Paulson's announcement was to signal to the markets that the United States government was not going to let the financial ship go down. Yes, it was just a three-page memo asking for authorization to spend hundreds of billions of taxpayer dollars. Would more detail have been preferred? Yes. Did we have time? No. While the devil is typically in the details, in this case, the markets needed reassurance more than Congress needed details; otherwise Congress would be discussing the details of rebuilding the financial system as opposed to saving it.

While I do not support the idea of bank bailouts, they were the lesser of two evils. Without them, the entire financial system very likely would have collapsed, taking with it the global economy, because financing is the lifeblood that keeps the economy functioning. The solutions contained in this section are intended to reduce the frequency of having to choose among those two options in the future.

Financial Booms and Busts Equal Faster Profits for Some

Given the massive damage that an unstable financial system can do, why wouldn't everyone support measures to moderate financial booms and busts? Why, instead, do people come up with rationalizations for maintaining the status quo in our financial system? Because some can make a lot more money in a much shorter period under the current system.

Remember how today's bank executive compensation system is based on the quantity of loans they make? Under that scenario, you wouldn't want anything that curtails loan volume; the bigger the boom, the better. If you are a bank executive with significant stock options, you also want greater financial booms because you make more money in a shorter period than if you must wait for your stock values to grow at a measured, sustainable pace. Under the financial boom and bust scenario, you can make so much money during the boom that you don't have to worry about the bust. Even if there is a subsequent bust, it doesn't matter because you've already made your money, while the rest of us are stuck with the pain of the financial bust, and none of the outsized profits and bonuses. That is why not everyone supports measures to moderate financial booms and busts. Those who work against moderating booms and busts are also the ones with the greatest financial capacity to exert disproportionate influence on the legislative process through campaign contributions.

While I do not support the idea of bank bailouts, they were the lesser of two evils.

Why, instead, do people come up with rationalizations for maintaining the status quo in our financial system? Because some can make a lot more money in a much shorter period under the current system.

SECTION IV

EXPANDING THE AMERICAN MIDDLE CLASS

26. EIGHT MILLION FEWER PRODUCERS

One of the most (it not the most) valuable assets of any country is its labor force. Why? The more goods and services a country produces, the wealthier it is. The quantity of goods and services produced depends on several factors, including its labor force. While it is not a new idea, it is critical to restate that the more goods and services a country produces, the wealthier its citizens are, and this depends on the country's labor force.

One way for USA Inc. to produce more goods and services is by increasing the utilization rate of its labor force. This is similar to a company producing more by increasing the utilization rate of its equipment. The labor force participation rate is a good metric to measure labor force utilization. As we saw previously, it measures the size of the labor force compared to the size of the working-age population. It is important to note that some may not be in the labor force because they are in school or retired, so you will not have a 100 percent participation rate, and it will naturally decline as more and more baby boomers move into retirement. It also declines during recessions as more people go back to school.

If production equals wealth and production relies on labor, the goal is to for USA Inc. to maximize its labor force utilization rate. This would move USA Inc. closer to its potential economic output. How important is increasing the utilization rate? Consider this: How many towns that have seen their labor force participation rates plummet are thriving? Or consider this: While not included when calculating the labor force participation rate, how much more prosperous would USA Inc. be if all those currently incarcerated were working? We would go from the shareholders of USA Inc. supporting an entire group to adding an entire group to USA Inc.'s productive capacity, increasing the wealth of USA Inc.'s shareholders. Increasing the labor force participation rate would also increase consumer purchasing power, a key for an economy like USA Inc.'s that is highly dependent on consumption for economic growth. It's straightforward: Increase labor force participation rates and increase economic prosperity.

Capitalizing on America's Untapped Human Capital

Since peaking in 2000 at 67.3 percent, the labor force participation rate of USA Inc. has steadily fallen to 63.1 percent, as of the end of 2018.[154] The decrease may not seem substantial, but when you look at the size of the working-age population of 206 million people as of December 2018, a 4 percent decrease from its peak in 2000 equates to 8.6 million more participants in the labor

154 "Civilian Labor Force Participation Rate: 16-64 Years," FRED.

force than we would otherwise have had.[155] Even among prime-age workers, men and women ages twenty-five to fifty-four, the labor force participation rate has fallen from its peak of 84.6 percent in 1999 to 82.3 percent in 2018.[156] These potential workers are not contributing to USA Inc.; they are not working, earning income, and adding to the productivity of USA Inc.

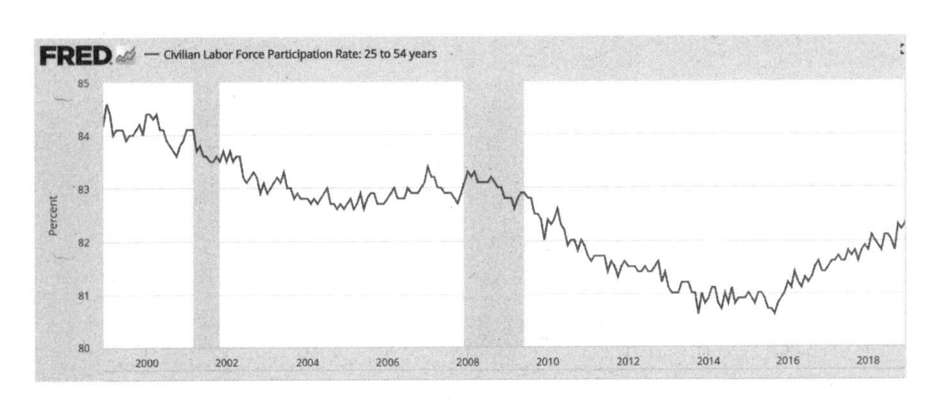

Source: Federal Reserve Bank of St. Louis

Increasing the utilization rate of USA Inc.'s human capital begins with identifying the segments of workers within the labor force having lower labor force participation rates, and most importantly, taking the steps necessary to increase their utilization rates.

---

155 "Civilian Labor Force Participation Rate: 25-54 Years," FRED.

156 "Working Age Population: Aged 15-64: All Persons for the United States," FRED.

27. NOT WHO YOU MIGHT EXPECT

A study conducted by Didem Tüzemen and the Federal Reserve Bank of Kansas City titled "Why Are Prime Age Men Vanishing from the Labor Force?" analyzed changes in the labor force participation rates from 1996 to 2017. The study found that labor force participation rates for prime-age men ages twenty-five to fifty-four varied significantly when segmented by education level. From 1996 to 2016, the labor force participation rate for prime-age male workers of all education levels decreased substantially, from 91.8 percent to 88.6 percent.[157] In 1996, 4.6 million prime-age male workers did not participate in the labor force and by 2016, this figure had increased to 7.1 million.[158] From 1996 to 2016, for those with less than a high school degree, the labor force participation rate decreased from 81.7 percent to 79.7 percent, while those with a high school degree but no college saw their labor force participation rate decline the most, from 91.2 percent to 85.1 percent. While somewhat better but still a significant decline, those with some college saw a reduction from 93.2 percent to 89 percent, and those with a college degree also saw a decline but much less, going from 95.9 percent to 94 percent.[159]

157 Didem Tüzemen, "Why Are Prime Age Men Vanishing from the Labor Force?" Federal Reserve Bank of Kansas City, *Economic Review*, First Quarter 2018.

158 Ibid.

159 Ibid.

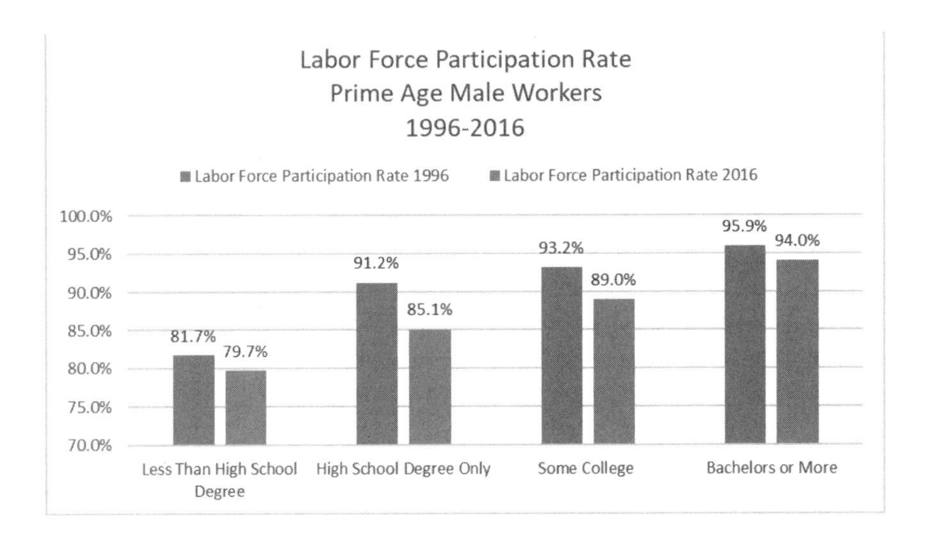

It is highly concerning that labor force participation rates dropped across all education levels. The universal decline indicates a pervasive problem, not just an isolated problem. What is most instructive is that it is not those *without* a high school degree, but those *with* a high school degree but not a college degree experienced the largest decreases in labor force participation rates, a sizable 6.2 percentage point decline. Why? Because it allows us to focus our efforts where the primary problem is occurring—where the most opportunity for improvement is.

28. THE ENDANGERED MIDDLE-SKILL JOB

The workers with a high school degree experiencing the greatest decline in labor force participation primarily hold jobs that fall in the middle-skill job category. Importantly, these also happen to be the very jobs that, as we saw in Myth #7 in Part

Three, Section II, "Winning the Game of Global Trade," some say are okay to continue sending overseas. Try telling that to this group of workers seeing their labor force participation rates decline and see how that goes over. Compare this to President Trump's message during the 2016 presidential campaign that acknowledged the damage being done to this segment of our labor force by global trade policies based on the myth that it is okay to send more middle-skill jobs overseas. This partially explains how many counties which previously voted for President Obama could subsequently vote for Trump: He understood that this segment of the population was disproportionately suffering economically, and individual economic hardship "trumped" party ideology.

"What is most instructive is that it is not those *without* a high school degree, but those *with* a high school degree but not a college degree that experienced the largest decreases in their labor force participation rates.

While it may be surprising at first glance, the large declines in labor force participation rates among those with high school degrees and occupying middle-skill level jobs make sense when examining which jobs in USA Inc. are disappearing the fastest. A different study conducted by Tüzemen and the Federal Reserve Bank of Kansas City titled "The Vanishing Middle: Job Polarization and Workers' Response to the Decline in Middle-Skill Jobs" analyzed changes in the composition of jobs in the economy from 1983 to 2012, based on the skill level required for the job. The study divided jobs in the economy into three categories: low-skill, middle-skill, and high-skill. Low-skill jobs are typically entry-level minimum wage jobs that require no formal education and are often in occupations that are physically demanding and cannot be automated easily, such as food preparation and cleaning services.[160] The share of low-skill jobs in the economy *increased* from 15 percent to 18 percent from 1983 to 2012.[161] High-skill jobs typically require a bachelor's degree as a minimum educational requirement and are often in occupations that require analytical ability, problem solving, and creativity, such as managerial, professional, and technical occupations.[162] The share of these jobs also *increased* from 26 percent to 37 percent from 1983 to 2012.[163] Middle-skill jobs are typically held by workers with a high school degree or some college education that did not end with a bachelor's degree, such as an associate's degree or credential, and are often in occupations where the workers perform routine tasks that are procedural and rule-based, such as sales, office and administrative support, production, manufacturing, construction, transportation, and material moving.[164] This is where the largest shift in job composition occurred. Middle-skill jobs now comprise less than half of all jobs, decreasing significantly from 59 percent to 45 percent of all jobs from 1983 to 2012.[165]

---

160 Didem Tüzemen and Jonathan Willis, "The Vanishing Middle: Job Polarization and Workers' Response to the Decline in Middle-Skill Jobs," Federal Reserve Bank of Kansas City, *Economic Review*, First Quarter 2013.

161 Ibid.

162 Ibid.

163 Ibid.

164 Ibid.

165 Ibid.

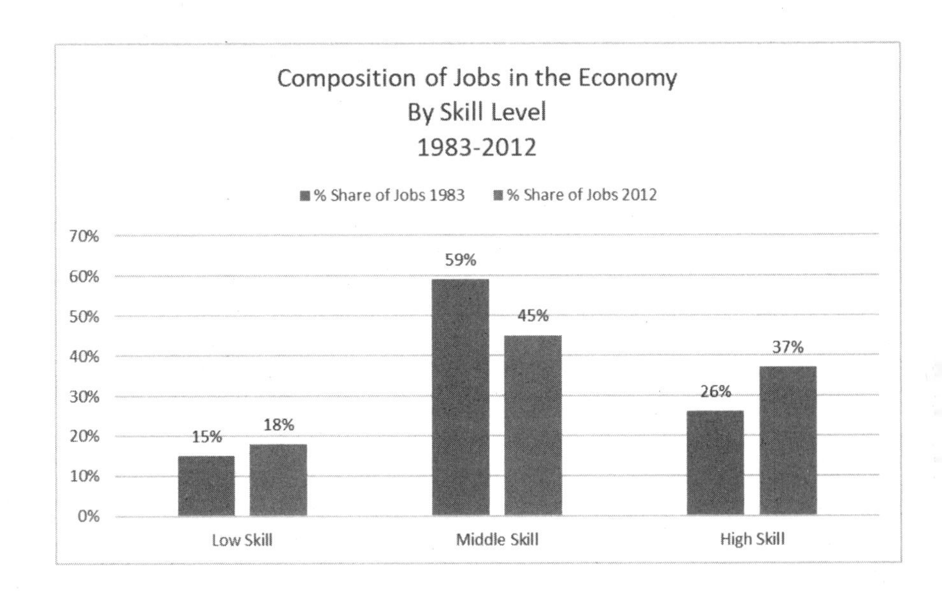

Where did the jobs go? Sixty-six percent of this decline in middle-skill jobs occurred because the demand for labor within each sector shifted from middle-skill jobs into both high- and low-skill jobs.[166] The other 33 percent of the shift from middle-skill jobs occurred due to the seismic decline of middle-skill jobs in the manufacturing sector without a commensurate increase in high- or low-skill jobs within the manufacturing sector.[167]

Middle-skill jobs now comprise less than half of all jobs.

166 Ibid.
167 Ibid.

The same study determined that in 1983, manufacturing jobs made up 22 percent of the total jobs in the economy and that, by 2012, the number of manufacturing jobs had decreased to only 11 percent of the total jobs in the economy.[168] Said differently, as a share of total jobs in the economy, manufacturing experienced a 100 percent decrease from 1983 to 2012. Looking at more recent declines, in 2000 the total number of manufacturing jobs was 17 million; by 2018 that had fallen to 12 million, a loss of 5 million or 34 percent.[169] In the 2007-2009 recession alone, the number of manufacturing jobs decreased by 1.5 million and by 2010, 57.8 percent of these 1.5 million workers (906,304) became classified as long-term unemployed or gave up looking for work and fell out of the labor force.[170] This contributed to not only to the substantial decrease in labor force participation rates, but critical middle-skill jobs.

Has this decline in middle-skill jobs affected male and female workers equally? The answer is no. The study found that a significant portion of female workers responded to the decline in middle-skill jobs by increasing their level of education and attaining higher-skill jobs to a greater degree than male workers. Those male workers saw a more modest increase in their education level and attainment of higher-skill jobs, with an equal shift into both high- and low-skill jobs.[171] This applies only to those workers who remained

---

168 Ibid.

169 Ibid.

170 "All Employees: Manufacturing," FRED, Dec. 7, 2018.

171 "Displaced Workers by Industry: Reemployment Rates, All Displaced Workers, by Industry," U.S. Bureau of Labor Statistics, January 2010.

in the labor force. As we have seen from the previous data, a significant number of workers simply fell out of the labor force. This is a fundamental weakness of USA Inc., because reduced labor force participation constrains not only its near-term economic output potential but also the stability of its financial system, as lenders are left with fewer qualified borrowers. And as we saw with the subprime mortgage crisis and are currently seeing with subprime credit card lending and auto loans, when lenders run out of prime borrowers, they simply lend more to subprime borrowers—putting the entire financial system at risk. Declining labor force participation rates are not just making our economy weaker; they are weakening the stability of our financial system.

A partial explanation for the unequal shift by male and female workers can be seen by examining the industries experiencing the largest job gains and losses over the past decades. The manufacturing industry experienced the largest decrease in jobs since 2000, while the health care sector has experienced the largest increase in jobs since 2000. This is important because manufacturing is a male-dominated occupation while the health care industry is a female-dominated occupation. In 2017, only 29 percent of manufacturing jobs were held by women, while 78 percent of health-care-related jobs were held by women.[172]

> Declining labor force participation rates don't just make our economy weaker; they are weakening the stability of our financial system.

172 Tüzemen and Willis, "The Vanishing Middle."

Male workers with *middle-skill* and *middle education* are suffering the most. This should also not be surprising, given that, as we saw in Myth #7 in Part Three, Section II, "Winning the Game of Global Trade," trade policy was based on the myth that it was okay to send more and more manufacturing jobs overseas. It turns out that, as we were sending more and more middle-skill jobs overseas, these middle jobs were not always replaced with higher-skill jobs, as promised, but an increasing number of low-skill jobs. Meanwhile, some middle-skill workers never even made it back into the workforce.

These middle jobs were not always replaced with higher-skill jobs, as promised, but an increasing number of low-skill jobs. Meanwhile, some middle-skill workers never even made it back into the workforce.

Some workers were able to adapt to the reduction in middle-skill jobs by increasing their level of education and acquiring higher-skill jobs. However, a more significant portion of workers either took lower-skill and, therefore, lower-paying jobs, or simply exited the labor force and are no longer contributing to the productive capacity of USA Inc. This can be clearly and painfully seen in the depressing state of many towns comprising the manufacturing core of USA Inc.

One note on automation and its contribution to the decrease in middle-skill jobs and, particularly, manufacturing jobs: While automation has certainly contributed to the decrease in the number of manufacturing jobs, concluding that we don't need to focus on the plant closings sending more of these jobs overseas is misinformed at best and deceptive at worst. Let's say that more than half of the middle-skill jobs lost were lost due to automation. Why in the world would you make it worse by choosing to send more of those jobs overseas? In a normal world, you would do the exact opposite. You would do everything you could to keep plants from closing in the U.S.to not make the problem worse. Instead, trade policy since WWII has been adding insult to injury to the workers suffering the effects of automation.

To those who would tell the middle-skill, middle-education worker that this is all the price of lower-priced goods or the cost of advancing foreign policy, it is time we tell them—we can do better than that. And if those currently promoting and justifying the trade and foreign policies that are contributing to the loss of middle-skill jobs can't do any better, then they better make room for those who can, because surely, we can do better.

While the magnitude of the loss of middle-skill jobs is staggering and concerning, it is the very magnitude of the losses that makes it the segment of our labor force where there is the greatest room for improvement. It is the area of our workforce where we should be marshaling and concentrating our resources just as we would in combating a medical epidemic, because what the middle-skill worker is experiencing is an epidemic of shrinking job opportunities. And as we saw in the section on global trade, with other countries rapidly advancing their technological capabilities, it is an epidemic that can easily spread to higher-skill jobs.

The political candidates who understand that it is the middle-skill workers who have lost their foothold on the American dream *and* that this is where the greatest opportunity for improvement is will be a step ahead in 2020. If you doubt this, consider Trump's success in the middle of the country, where middle-skill workers have been devastated.

29. INCREASING THE UTILIZATION RATE OF USA INC.'S HUMAN CAPITAL

Despite the significant decline in the number of middle-skill jobs typically held by workers who have a high school degree, this segment still represents the largest share of the jobs in the economy, 45 percent according to a U.S. Bureau of Labor Statistics report dated October 14, 2018, "Middle-Skill Jobs Decline as U.S. Labor Market Becomes More Polarized." It is a major problem for USA Inc. when the segment of jobs constituting the largest share of employment in the economy is declining at the fastest rate.

> It is a major problem for USA Inc. when the segment of jobs constituting the largest share of employment in the economy is declining at the fastest rate.

If a company had its largest share of equipment increasingly sitting idle at the fastest pace, it would do something about it and would certainly stop doing the things making it worse. Instead, our past CEOs and managers of USA Inc. made it worse by in effect saying it's okay if we close more plants and send more jobs overseas. Worse still, members of the 115th Congress compounded the situation by eliminating taxes on goods made overseas, encouraging companies to move plants and jobs overseas. Brilliant! Make it even more financially advantageous to produce overseas! Seriously?! We can do better, much better. In addition to basing future trade and tax policy on the reality that we can't afford to send more of these jobs overseas, there are other steps we can take to both preserve these jobs and increase the number of these workers who become qualified for higher-skill, higher-paying jobs.

An academic paper titled "Fostering and Measuring Skills: Interventions That Improve Character and Cognition," by James J. Heckman and Tim Kautz with the National Bureau of Economic Research, analyzed the needs of employers and found evidence of the importance of labor market skills beyond the often-thought-of technical skills. In a survey of 3,200 employers in four large metropolitan areas conducted in the 1990s, the employers reported that non-technical, sometimes referred to as character-related success skills such as responsibility, integrity, and self-management, are equally as important, if not more important, than basic technical skills.[173] These non-technical skills are especially critical for entry-level and hourly workers, as these jobs do not require significant amounts of technical skills.[174] Character skills are critical to succeed in the labor market, regardless of the minimum educational requirement.

The paper also reviewed other studies that looked at the experience of employers taken from a national sample across the United States in 1996 and found that 69 percent of these employers reported rejecting hourly applicants because they lacked basic character skills, such as showing up every day, coming to work on time, and having a strong work ethic. This is more than double

173 James J. Heckman and Tim Kautz, "Fostering and Measuring Skills: Interventions That Improve Character and Cognition," National Bureau of Economic Research Working Paper No. 19656, December 2013.

174 Ibid.

the number of applicants rejected due to inadequate reading and writing skills.[175] In another study conducted in 2007, the authors examined a survey of employers in Washington State and found that about 60 percent of the employers had difficulty in hiring workers.[176] Why? Not so much because of a lack of technical skills. In fact, they experienced less difficulty finding workers with adequate reading, writing, and math skills than finding those with the teamwork, communication and adaptability skills, positive work habits, and willingness to accept supervision that are required to succeed in the labor market.[177] While it is the technical skills that get all the media attention, the workers of USA Inc. are entering the workforce without the essential non-technical work-related success skills needed to secure and succeed in a job.

The workers of USA Inc. are entering the workforce without having developed the essential non-technical work-related success skills needed to secure and succeed in a job.

Career Mentoring Is an ROI Accelerator

The authors of the previously mentioned paper *Fostering and Measuring Skills* analyzed several programs focused on preparing students for the labor market. The most successful of these programs incorporates important aspects of employment into traditional education by breaking down the separation between school and

175 Ibid.
176 Ibid.
177 Ibid.

work that often characterizes American education.[178] In previous decades, new workers in the labor market took apprenticeships and jobs in which they were supervised and mentored by more experienced workers. Mentoring involved teaching the critical non-technical skills that are critical for success in the work environment, such as showing up for work, cooperating with co-workers, and perseverance.

The authors also examined a study of high school students who participated in a youth apprenticeship program. The study found that students in the program achieved earnings levels substantially higher than youth not in the program.[179] Well-structured, career-focused programs featuring both career-specific training and mentoring have been shown to enhance technical and work-related success skills that are critical for success in the work environment. Participants in these programs develop expertise in an occupation as well as in problem-solving, teamwork and the ability to take direction, take initiative, acquire self-confidence, and see themselves as able to meet or exceed the required standards of a discipline.[180] Experienced mentors within the profession focus the apprentices' attention and control the tasks to keep them challenging yet constructive.[181]

Fostering workplaces as learning environments is motivated by evidence of the importance of non-technical character skills, such as self-management, persistence, and a strong work ethic.[182]

178 Ibid.
179 Ibid.
180 Ibid.
181 Ibid.
182 Ibid.

Workplace-oriented training can help workers attain development goals such as personal autonomy, efficacy, motivation, realism, optimism, and knowledge of vocations. It also facilitates matching between workers and firms and motivates workers to acquire relevant academic and work-related success skills.[183] This is why the combination of career and professional mentoring is a crucial element of training programs for current middle-skill workers in the labor market as well as future workers of USA Inc.

Career Academies is one example of a labor market training program modeled after this approach that was examined by the authors. The program improves earnings for males in the long run without having to improve educational attainment or scores on achievement tests.[184] Career Academies likely improves the essential skills necessary to succeed in the work environment by providing internships that teach students the importance of a strong work ethic and self-management, along with other occupation-related skills that improve their labor market preparation. Programs that integrate school and work not only motivate workers to learn relevant academic material but also integrate workers into the larger society and teach them the skills valued in the workplace and in society at large.[185]

Short career-focused programs, associate's degree and credential programs that provide occupation-specific training, development, and mentorship are key components in increasing the near-term human capital utilization rate of USA Inc. They target the most underutilized group of workers, those with middle-education levels

---

183 Ibid.

184 Ibid.

185 Ibid.

who primarily hold jobs requiring a high school degree or some college education as a minimum requirement. These programs teach the skills necessary for middle-skill workers to acquire and excel in middle-skill/education jobs.

Even if the number of high-skill jobs does increase, it will be of little help to middle-skill workers if they do not have the technical and non-technical skills that will allow them to succeed in the new high-skill jobs. Work-based education will provide occupation-specific training and development that will allow these workers to become proficient in a field, ideally in a field that will not be automated out of existence. Career mentoring will provide these workers with essential training to develop the skills necessary to succeed in the work environment, including hard work, determination, persistence, and self-management.

Providing middle-skill level workers with these non-technical skills in addition to the technical skills needed to succeed in the workforce would not only benefit them, but also the shareholders of USA Inc. through greater labor force participation rates among this segment. It would drive greater economic output of USA Inc.: increased consumer purchasing, which comprises 70 percent of GDP, and reduced welfare costs, among other economic benefits. USA Inc. would be wise to also prepare both current workers and future high school graduates through both technical and essential non-technical skills, which can be learned through professional mentoring education programs.

Expanding the Middle Class Solution #1**:** Support programs proven to successfully teach and enhance the technical and work-related success skills that are critical for success in the work environment.

Expanding the Middle Class Solution #2: Annually review program results measuring improvement in hiring and retention rates; pay increases as compared to pay before entering the program; and employer satisfaction, increasing money for programs achieving the desired results and eliminating funding for programs not achieving required results.

30. MAXIMIZING THE ROI ON TOMORROW'S WORKFORCE

Increasing the Productivity and Earnings Potential of the Children of Today's Middle- and Lower-Skill Workers

How do we increase the odds that the children of today's middle- and lower-skill workers are more productive and earn more than their parents? Increase their access to effective post-high-school education. Why should we care? Why should we work to ensure these children have access to the post-high-school education necessary to qualify for these jobs?

First, it will help increase the labor force participation rate by reducing the portion of our labor force that is dependent on the shrinking pool of middle-skill jobs. Second, USA Inc. will see a significant return on investment as these future workers' increased wages and productivity associated with higher-skill jobs will increase USA Inc.'s potential economic output and overall prosperity. Remember the list of benefits flowing from increasing the number of higher-paying jobs noted earlier in the book? Some of these included higher home values, reduced welfare spending, lower crime and incarceration rates, rising stock values, and being able to afford greater military spending. Even if we generate more of these jobs, we still need to ensure that more of USA Inc.'s labor force is prepared and qualified for them. Additionally, investing in the programs necessary to prepare more of our labor force for these jobs through increased access to the most effective post-high-school education would go a long way toward increasing the earnings potential and financial stability of our workforce. This is critical given that USA Inc.'s workforce makes up the customers the companies rely on and approximately 70 percent of GDP is comprised of personal consumption, consumption which relies on the earnings of our workforce.

USA Inc.'s workforce makes up the customers the companies rely on and approximately 70 percent of GDP is comprised of personal consumption, consumption which relies on the earnings of our workforce.

31. EDUCATION'S POWERFUL ROLE IN INTERGENERATIONAL MOBILITY

An academic paper titled "Mobility Report Cards: The Role of Colleges in Intergenerational Mobility," by Raj Chetty et al., analyzes the impact of colleges on promoting upward intergenerational mobility. Intergenerational mobility is the extent to which a child's income or earnings differ from those of their parents. In a promising sign, students who come from low-income families have post-college outcomes similar to students from high-income families who attend the same college.[186] This indicates the possibility

186 Raj Chetty, John N. Friedman, Emmanuel Saez, Nicholas Turner, and Danny Yagan, "Mobility Report Cards: The Role of Colleges in Intergenerational Mobility," National Bureau of Economic Research Working Paper 23618, July 2017, 1-2.

to improve the economic outcomes of the children of middle- and lower-skill workers.

The authors analyzed the role and significance of colleges in promoting upward intergenerational income mobility. They evaluated how successful each college is at preparing its students for the labor market, with success based on the students' ability to earn a higher income than their parents.[187]

The authors calculated intergenerational mobility rates for each college using a) the percentage of low-income students from each college who successfully moved from the bottom income quintile to the top income quintile, and b) the level of access each college provided to low-income students. The authors found that the colleges having the highest upward mobility rates—that is, those that offer both high mobility rates and high levels of access—are typically mid-tier public institutions, not the elite academic institutions that often come to mind. Why is this?

While some colleges may have similar success rates in moving their low-income students from the bottom income quintile to the top quintile, there are very large differences in access.[188] The "Ivy-Plus" colleges have the highest success rates in moving low-income students to higher-income levels, with almost 60 percent of students from the bottom quintile of the income distribution reaching the top quintile. However, they are also highly selective, reducing their mobility rates. Conversely, certain less selective universities have comparable success rates to the Ivy-Plus colleges in moving students from lower- to higher-income quintiles, and importantly, offer much higher levels of access to low-income families, generating

187 Ibid.
188 Ibid., 3.

greater mobility rates.[189] For example, the authors found that 51 percent of students from the bottom quintile of the income distribution reach the top quintile at the State University of New York at Stony Brook (SUNY-Stony Brook), which compares favorably to the 60 percent rate at the Ivy-Plus colleges. However, whereas 16.4 percent of students at SUNY-Stony Brook are from the bottom quintile of the income distribution, only 3.8 percent at the Ivy-Plus colleges are from the bottom income quintile. As a result, Stony Brook has an upward mobility rate of 8.4 percent, substantially higher than the 2.2 percent rate at the Ivy-Plus colleges. Colleges having the highest upward mobility rates—that is, those that offer both high success rates and high levels of access—are typically mid-tier public institutions.

> Colleges having the highest intergenerational mobility rates—that is, those that offer both high mobility rates and high levels of access—are typically mid-tier public institutions.

Many of the colleges with the highest rates of upward intergenerational mobility are public colleges, such as the California state colleges, SUNY-Stony Brook, City University of New York, other mid-tier public institutions, and a number of community colleges.[190] These colleges are less selective institutions in terms of observable student data such as SAT scores or high school GPAs, which suggests that these colleges could b For example, the authors found that 51 percent of students from the bottom e a key ingredient in producing large returns

189 Ibid.

190 Ibid., 5.

for students at significantly less cost than for-profit or private nonprofit colleges.[191]

These institutions are also often much less expensive, offering more educational success for the buck. Their mean annual instructional expenditure is approximately $8,000 per student, compared to the mean instructional expenditure at Ivy-Plus colleges of $54,000, which are often the focus of efforts to increase access to high-quality higher education.[192] These figures indicate that federal and state student aid would experience the highest return on investment for the shareholders of USA Inc., and the USA Inc.'s future workforce, by providing more aid to the public colleges with the highest mobility rates and less to those with lower mobility rates. The shareholders of USA Inc. can get a higher return on their investment if it considers mobility rates when allocating funding, not just the brand name of an institution.

Solution: Increase federal funding to the institutions having higher mobility rates while reducing funding to the institutions having lower mobility rates.

Federal Funding for the Most Effective Institutions Declining

The authors of the previously mentioned paper found that the number of children from low-income families attending college increased significantly since 2000, both in absolute numbers and as a share of total college enrollment. However, most of this increase occurred at for-profit institutions. Conversely, the share of students from low-income families at public colleges and private nonprofit

191 Ibid.

192 Ibid.

colleges did not change significantly.[193] Even at the Ivy-Plus colleges, which enacted substantial tuition reductions for lower income students during this period, the fraction of students from families at the bottom of the income distribution did not increase significantly.[194] However, the authors argue that this result does not imply that the increases in financial aid had no effect on access; absent these changes, the fraction of low-income students might have fallen, especially given that real incomes of low-income families fell due to widening inequality during the 2000s. Most importantly, the authors found that the fraction of students from low-income families attending institutions with the highest mobility rates, for example, SUNY-Stony Brook, California state colleges, and Glendale (California) Community College, *decreased* sharply since 2000.

> The fraction of students from low-income families attending the institutions with the highest mobility rates *decreased* sharply since 2000.

A possible explanation is that state funding for public colleges has been declining, while tuition costs have been increasing. It has been a decade since the Great Recession hit, and state spending on public colleges remains well below historic levels, despite recent increases in 2017. A paper titled "A Lost Decade in Higher Education Funding: State Cuts Have Driven Up Tuition and Reduced Quality," by Michael Mitchell et al. with the Center on Budget and Policy Priorities, found that state funding for public two-year community colleges and four-year colleges in the 2017 school year was nearly $9 billion below its 2008 level,

---

193 Ibid.
194 Ibid.

> State funding for public two-year community colleges and four-year colleges in the 2017 school year was nearly $9 billion below its 2008 level, after adjusting for inflation

after adjusting for inflation. That has contributed to higher tuition and reduced quality of education through less faculty, limited course offerings, and in some cases, the closing of campuses.[195]

While the number of students attending college continues to increase, the amount of state funding for colleges is less than it was ten years ago.

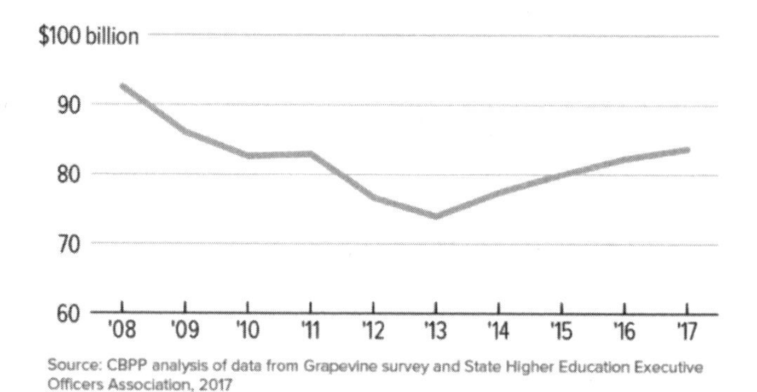

195 Michael Mitchell, Michael Leachman, and Kathleen Masterson, "A Lost Decade in Higher Education Funding: State Cuts Have Driven Up Tuition and Reduced Quality," Center on Budget and Policy Priorities, Aug. 23, 2017.

For the average student, increases in federal student aid and the availability of tax credits have not kept up, jeopardizing the ability of many to afford the college education that is necessary for their success in the labor market.[196]

Tuition Growth Has Vastly Outpaced Income Gains

Inflation-adjusted average tuition and fees at public four-year institutions and income for select groups (1973 = 100%)

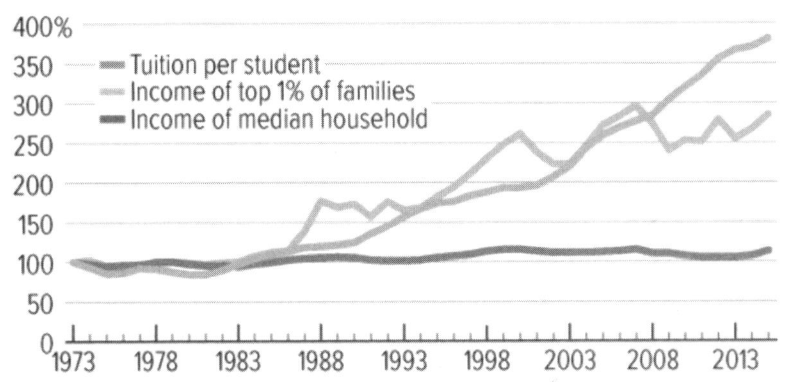

Source: Center on Budget and Policy Priorities based on the College Board and Census Bureau. Tuition per student and income levels, adjusted for inflation, as a percentage of 1973-1974 price levels. Years shown and income data are for the calendar year. Tuition data cover the school year beginning in the calendar year.

CENTER ON BUDGET AND POLICY PRIORITIES | CBPP.ORG

The authors found that the average state spent 16 percent less per student in 2017 than in 2008.

196 Ibid.

The average state spent 16 percent less per student in 2017 than in 2008.

Even though 2016 and 2017 saw modest increases in per-student state spending for thirty-six states, that rise has not come close to making up for the cuts seen during the recession. Per-student funding in these states increased by only $170, or 2.2 percent between 2016 and 2017.[197] Additionally, from 2008 to 2017, tuition at four-year public colleges increased by $2,484, or 35 percent, meaning these tuition increases have accelerated the long-term trend of college becoming less affordable.[198]

197 Ibid.

198 Ibid.

State Funding for Higher Education Remains Far Below Pre-Recession Levels in Most States

Percent change in state spending per student, inflation adjusted, 2008-2017

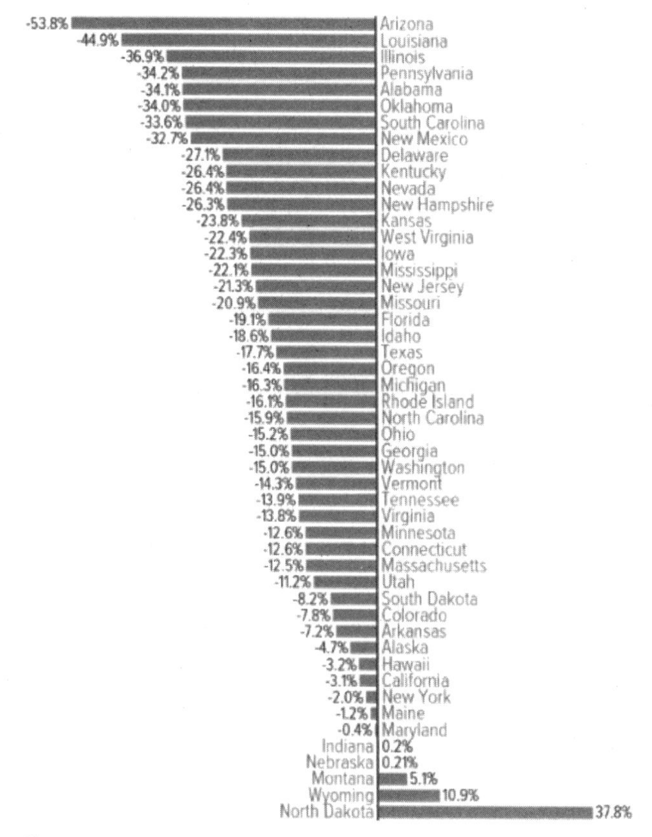

Note: Wisconsin was excluded because the data necessary to make a valid comparison are not available. Since enrollment data is only available through the 2015-16 school year, we have estimated enrollment for the 2016-17 school year using data from past years.

Source: CBPP calculations using the "Grapevine" higher education appropriations data from Illinois State University, enrollment and combined state and local funding data from the State Higher Education Executive Officers Association, and the Consumer Price Index, published by the Bureau of Labor Statistics. Illinois funding data is provided by Voices for Illinois Children.

CENTER ON BUDGET AND POLICY PRIORITIES | CBPP.OR

Tuition Has Increased Sharply at Public Colleges and Universities

Percent change in average tuition at public, four-year colleges, inflation adjusted, 2008-2017

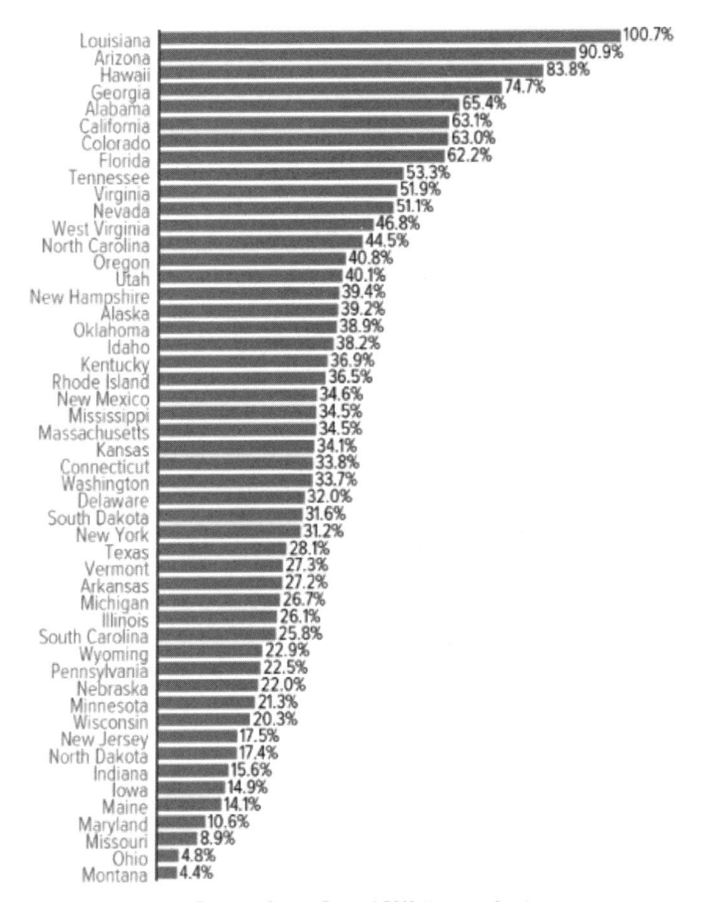

Source: College Board, "Trends in College Pricing," 2016. Years are fiscal years.

CENTER ON BUDGET AND POLICY PRIORITIES | CBPP.ORG

Increases in federal financial aid have helped some students offset about 70 percent of the average $2,500 tuition increase experienced by public colleges since 2008. However, because tuition increases have varied across states while federal grant amounts are uniform nationally, students in the states that experienced the highest tuition increases are likely still struggling to meet the substantial tuition increases at public colleges. Additionally, the increase in federal financial aid is now at risk. From the same paper, *A Lost Decade in Higher Education Funding*, the authors noted that in 2018, the House Appropriations Committee proposed a $3.3 billion cut to Pell Grants (federal grants aimed to help students from low-income families attend public colleges). Similarly, the House Budget Committee's 2018 budget resolution called for eliminating a significant portion of Pell Grant funding, proposing an 18 percent cut.[199]

The California State University (CSU) system, which contains some of the colleges with the highest rates of upward intergenerational mobility, is a clear example of an effective university system both experiencing decreased state funding and increasing tuition. In 2000, state spending per student at CSU schools was about $11,000. By 2015, state spending per student at CSU schools had decreased to about $6,800 on an inflation-adjusted basis.[200] Along with this decrease in state spending per student, tuition and fees at CSU schools have increased significantly. Since 1990, tuition and fees for CSU schools have more than tripled, after adjusting for inflation. That means students are paying an increasing share

199 Ibid.

200 Ibid., 19.

of higher education costs because declines in state support and increases in tuition and fees at CSU schools have shifted a larger share of education costs from the state to the students.[201]

Declining funding for the most effective institutions and increasing tuition costs makes ensuring tomorrow's workforce is qualified to fill higher-skill, higher-paying jobs even more challenging.

We are, in effect, saying, "Don't worry about us sending all the middle-skill jobs overseas. You can get the higher-skill, higher-paying jobs," only later to say, "Sorry, we are cutting the funding needed for you to be able to get the training, degrees, or certificates you need to be able to qualify for those jobs. You're welcome."

We are, in effect, saying, "Don't worry about us sending all the middle-skill jobs overseas. You can get the higher-skill, higher-paying jobs," only later to say, "Sorry, we are cutting the funding needed for you to be able to get the training, degrees, or certificates you need to be able to qualify for those jobs. You're welcome."

32. FOR EDUCATION OR PROFIT? THE TRUTH ABOUT FOR-PROFIT COLLEGES' TAXPAYER ROI

Proponents of for-profit colleges see them as the solution to providing workers with the skills they need to succeed in the labor market, but are they? Based on the spike in government spending going toward for-profit colleges, either our management incorrectly

201 Ibid.

thinks so or the increase reflects the effects of policy decisions driven by campaign donations and lobbying, not ROI.

A paper titled *For-Profit Higher Education: The Failure to Safeguard the Federal Investment and Ensure Student Success*, issued by the United States Senate Health, Education, Labor and Pensions Committee, analyzed the cost of colleges in the for-profit college sector and how these colleges' performance compared to traditional public colleges. They found that for-profit certificate programs and associate's degree programs cost, on average, four and a half times as much as comparable programs at community colleges in the same area, and bachelor's degree programs at for-profit colleges cost an average of 20 percent more than comparable programs at public colleges.[202] The average cost of a two-year associate's degree at a for-profit college is $35,000, while a two-year associate's degree at a public community college costs on average $8,300.

For-profit certificate programs and associate's degree programs cost, on average, four and a half times as much as comparable programs at community colleges in the same area.

The average cost of a four-year bachelor's degree at a for-profit college is $63,000, while a four-year bachelor's degree at a public college costs an average of $52,000. The average cost of a certificate program at a for-profit college is $19,000, while the average cost of a certificate program at a public college is $4,000.[203]

202 "For-Profit Education: The Failure to Safeguard the Federal Investment and Ensure Student Success," United States Senate Health, Education, Labor and Pensions Committee, July 30, 2012, 36.

203 Ibid.

Not surprisingly, given the exorbitant costs, the paper also found that students at for-profit colleges leave school with more debt than students at public colleges, and that students at for-profit colleges are more likely to default on their loans after leaving school than students at public colleges. The median debt of the average student after leaving a for-profit college is $32,000, compared to $20,000 at public colleges.[204] The percent of students enrolled at for-profit colleges who take out student loans is 96 percent compared with 48 percent at public colleges and 13 percent at community colleges.[205] Additionally, students from for-profit colleges have higher default rates on their student loans than those from public colleges; 22 percent or slightly more than 1 in 5 students who attend a for-profit college default on their student loans, while 9 percent or 1 in 11 students who attend a nonprofit college default on their student loans.[206] Not only do more students take out loans at for-profit colleges relative to public colleges, but the size of their loans are larger due to the higher tuition costs.

In a clear misallocation of resources by USA Inc.'s managers and poor ROI for the American taxpayer, despite students attending for-profit colleges, leaving college with higher student debt and greater likelihood of defaulting on their loans, for-profit colleges are seeing their Pell Grant-related funds increase at a much higher rate than nonprofit colleges, such as traditional public and private colleges. The Pell Grant program, the largest federal grant program, created to assist needy students with college costs, totaled

---

204 Ibid., 113

205 Ibid.

206 Ibid., 114.

$8 billion in 2000 and jumped to $30 billion in 2009.[207] During that period, the amount of Pell Grant funds collected by for-profit colleges increased from $1.1 billion to $7.5 billion, an increase of 581 percent, while the amount of Pell Grant funds collected by nonprofit colleges increased from $6.9 billion to $22.3 billion, an increase of 223 percent.[208] It is important to keep in mind that, while the overall amount of funds going towards nonprofit colleges is larger, nonprofit colleges also enroll far more students than for-profit colleges. In 2016, total undergraduate enrollment in degree-seeking postsecondary colleges across both for-profit and nonprofit colleges was 16.9 million students. And of the total undergraduate students, 15.9 million were enrolled at nonprofit colleges, while only 1 million were enrolled at for-profit colleges.[209] This means that, on a per-student basis, for-profit colleges receive far greater amounts of federal Pell Grant funding than nonprofit colleges. In 2016, while nonprofit colleges received approximately $1,402 per student in federal Pell Grant funding, for-profit colleges received more than five times as much, at approximately $7,500 per student.

> In 2016, while nonprofit colleges received approximately $1,402 per student in Pell Grant funding, for-profit colleges received more than five times as much, at approximately $7,500 per student.

207 Ibid., 25.

208 Ibid.

209 "Undergraduate Enrollment," National Center for Education Statistics, Figure 4, May 2018.

It should come as no surprise, then, that for-profit college enrollment is growing at a much faster rate. Between 2000 and 2016, undergraduate enrollment at for-profit colleges increased 127 percent, while undergraduate enrollment at nonprofit colleges increased only 26 percent.[210] Thanks to Congress, more dollars are being allocated to the institutions, namely for-profit colleges, that, as we will see, are getting the worst results. While yet another example of USA Inc.'s taxpayer resources being managed badly, it is a significant opportunity to improve the ROI of Pell Grant funding.

Thanks to Congress, more dollars are being allocated to the institutions, namely for-profit colleges, that are getting the worst results. While yet another example of USA Inc.'s taxpayer resources being managed badly, it is a significant opportunity to improve the ROI of Pell Grant funding.

Expanding the Middle Class Solution #3: Increase Pell Grant funding to the most effective institutions while eliminating funding for the most costly and ineffective institutions.

Not only is the amount of federal aid going to for-profit colleges increasing at a far greater rate relative to nonprofit colleges, but for-profit colleges are increasingly reliant on federal financial aid for most of their revenue. In 2006, for-profit colleges derived 68 percent of their revenue from federal aid, and in 2010, that figure rose to 79 percent. Not surprisingly, for-profit education institutions collect a higher proportion of their revenues from federal

210 Ibid.

aid funds than most nonprofit colleges.[211] In 2010, for-profit colleges derived a surprising 79 percent of their revenue from federal aid. Why surprising? Because, as we will see, their performance is far inferior to non-profit institutions.

In 2010, for-profit colleges derived a questionable 79 percent of their revenue from federal aid. Why questionable? Because, as we will see, their performance is far inferior to nonprofit institutions.

The Problem with For-Profit Colleges

Pell Grants are investments, made by the shareholders of USA Inc. through their tax dollars, in the students and future workers of USA Inc. This investment is intended to pay returns to taxpayers and society by giving low- and middle-income families access to effective higher education and employment opportunities, thereby increasing their potential contributions to USA Inc. by expanding the tax base and decreasing the welfare base. However, students who go to for-profit colleges often do not achieve better outcomes than their counterparts who did not go to college, ending up instead with substantial debt burdens and often not completing the programs. USA Inc. is not earning an acceptable return on its investment from for-profit colleges.

Students at for-profit colleges are far more likely to leave school without earning a degree than students at public colleges. Of the students who enrolled at for-profit colleges in every type of program

211 "For-Profit Education," Senate.

for the 2008-2009 academic year, only 18 percent had completed their degree or certificate by the 2010-2011 academic year; 27 percent were still enrolled in their program; and 54 percent had dropped out.[212] After two years of school, 62 percent of students in associate's degree programs and 54 percent of students in bachelor's degree programs at for-profit colleges had dropped out without earning a degree, while 38 percent of students enrolled in certificate programs at for-profit colleges had dropped out without earning the certificate.[213] When comparing different types of programs at for-profit colleges, bachelor's and associate's degree programs have significantly worse retention rates and are far less successful at ensuring that students leave college with a degree, compared with certificate programs at for-profit colleges.

Completing a program and receiving a degree or certificate is the student's first step towards securing employment and paying off their student loans. As such, the retention and completion rates of colleges indicate a college's likelihood of providing an education to its students. We just saw from the data that 54 percent of students who started at for-profit colleges in bachelor degree programs in 2008 left without a degree by 2010. Additionally, only 22 percent of bachelor's-degree-seeking students complete and earn the degree at for-profit colleges, while 66 percent of bachelor's-degree-seeking students complete and earn the degree at nonprofit colleges, such as public colleges.[214] For-profit colleges do a far worse job of ensuring their students complete and earn a bachelor's degree compared to nonprofit colleges.

---

212 Ibid.

213 Ibid.

214 Ibid.

Completion rates of associate's degree programs are not quite as clear-cut. In 2004, 22 percent of community college students seeking an associate's degree completed and earned the degree, while 28 percent did at for-profit colleges.[215] While community colleges and for-profit colleges have similar retention rates for associate's-degree-seeking students, the significantly higher cost of for-profit programs makes them far riskier for both the students enrolled in the programs and the taxpayers who are paying for the federal funds these students receive. For-profit colleges are more expensive, forcing more for-profit students to borrow, and to borrow higher amounts. We saw earlier that 96 percent of students at for-profit colleges borrow to attend, while only 13 percent of students at community colleges do so. This means that the expense and risk of attempting but failing to earn a degree or certificate is much greater at for-profit colleges, while most community college students have little or no debt.[216]

> Only 22 percent of bachelor's-degree-seeking students complete and earn the degree at for-profit colleges, while 66 percent of bachelor's-degree-seeking students complete and earn the degree at nonprofit colleges, such as public colleges.

> The expense and risk of attempting but failing to earn a degree or certificate is much greater at for-profit colleges, while most community college students have little or no debt.

215 Ibid.

216 Ibid.

We also saw that tuition costs are significantly higher at for-profit colleges. Taxpayers of USA Inc. who are helping to fund the education of future workers would expect that this higher cost would be associated with higher spending on education-related expenses per student and would provide a higher quality of education. Don't we wish. Some for-profits dedicate up to 30 percent to marketing and recruiting, retain a large percentage of revenue as pretax profit, pay their executives far more than other colleges, and divert significant sums to nonacademic activities such as lobbying.[217]

After spending on marketing, recruiting, and other nonacademic activities such as lobbying, the amount that publicly traded for-profit education companies spend per student ranges between $800 and $3,500 per year, with the average amount spent being $2,000.[218] This is far less than the $8,000 average spent per student per year at public state colleges, the schools with the highest upward intergenerational mobility rates. Public colleges spend far more per student on education-related expenses than for-profit colleges. Additionally, we saw that for-profit colleges rely far more on federal and state student aid as their source of revenue. For-profit colleges have significantly higher tuition costs than public colleges, causing their students to borrow more frequently and at much higher amounts than at public colleges. That means for-profit colleges require significantly more federal and state funding to support their students and themselves. Yet for-profit colleges are spending significantly less per student on education-related expenses, expenses that increase the educational quality for their students, than public

217 Ibid.
218 Ibid.

colleges do. *For-profit colleges are providing a far inferior return on investment to the shareholders of USA Inc. and students, relative to the return on investment in public colleges.*

> For-profit colleges are providing a far inferior return on investment to the shareholders of USA Inc. and students, relative to the return on investment in public colleges.

If for-profit colleges are not a good investment relative to public colleges having better success rates and lower costs, why has enrollment at for-profit colleges grown so fast? In a paper titled "For-Profit Colleges," by David Deming et al. of Harvard in conjunction with the National Bureau of Economic Research, the authors suggest that students may view for-profit programs as better preparation for the labor market, because they provide many short, occupation-specific certificate and associate's degree programs that provide technical training, which can be applied directly to a job after completion.[219] However, the authors find that students enrolled in for-profit programs that are growing in demand (for example, many certificate and associate's degree programs in the health care profession) have worse outcomes (higher unemployment rates and lower wage rates) than community college students in similar programs. Based on these results, they concluded that the focus of for-profits on providing programs for fast-growing occupations does not explain why a student would choose to attend a for-profit college *if* the student also had access

219 David Deming, Claudia Goldin, and Lawrence Katz, "For-Profit Colleges," *Future of Children* 23, no. 1 (Spring 2013): 143.

to a comparable public college. Additional analysis included in the paper and outlined below provides some insights into this mystery.

First, although community colleges may provide an equal or better education at lower cost, demand for higher education is outpacing state funding. This results in students who might otherwise qualify for community college being weeded out due to capacity constraints, leaving for-profit colleges as their only option.[220]

> This results in students who might otherwise qualify for community college being weeded out due to capacity constraints, leaving for-profit colleges as their only option.

Students are turned away not because the community colleges are too selective, but because the colleges do not have the funding to support the increased demand. Therefore, the choice these students face is often to either attend a for-profit college or not attend college at all. Add in the reductions in college funding we saw previously, and we are crowding out students from the more effective public colleges and into the lower ROI for-profit schools, to the detriment of both students and taxpayers.

Some may argue that the inferior outcomes at for-profit colleges may be partly due to their admitting significantly more students who are less qualified, and therefore, often will not succeed as much as those who attend public and private nonprofit colleges. There is evidence that this may not be the case.

220 Ibid., 157-158.

Add in the reductions in college funding we saw previously, and we are crowding out student from the more effective public colleges and into the lower ROI for-profit schools, to the detriment of both students and taxpayers.

The authors of *For-Profit Colleges* found that adjusting for student background characteristics, such as demographics, preparation, and pre-enrollment family resources, narrowed the gap in post-school employment and earnings outcomes but did not eliminate it. Students from for-profit colleges still had lower earnings and were more likely to be unemployed or not participating in the labor force six years after their initial enrollment.[221]

The authors found in an earlier paper titled "The For-Profit Postsecondary School Sector" that students from for-profit colleges also have substantially higher default rates, even when controlling for demographics, academic preparation, and pre-enrollment family resources such as family income.[222] In 2009, the default rate for students with $5,001 to $10,000 in cumulative federal student loans was 26 percent for students from for-profit colleges, 10 percent for students from community colleges, and 7 percent for students from public four-year colleges.[223] For those students with $10,001 to $20,000 in debt, the default rate was 16 percent for students from for-profit colleges, 3 percent for students from

221 Ibid., 142.

222 David J. Deming, Claudia Goldin, and Lawrence F. Katz, The For-Profit Postsecondary School Sector: Nimble Critters or Agile Predators?" *National Bureau of Economic Research working paper*

223 Ibid.

community colleges, and 2 percent for students from four-year public colleges.[224]

Loan default rates remained substantially higher for students attending for-profit colleges than for comparable students attending public and private nonprofit colleges. The authors found that, six years after initial enrollment, students in for-profit colleges were more likely to be unemployed and to have experienced substantial unemployment, being unemployed more than three months.[225] While they did find that for-profit schools do slightly better in terms of retention and completion rates for short, one-year, certificate programs, students from for-profit colleges in these programs end up with higher debt burdens and experience greater unemployment after leaving the program than comparable students from public colleges.[226]

In a paper titled "Evaluating Student Outcomes at For-Profit Colleges," by Kevin Lang and Russell Weinstein with the National Bureau of Economic Research, the authors found that students at for-profit colleges who had completed a certificate program had no increase in their earnings compared with students who began the program but did not complete it.[227] Additionally, students who completed an associate's degree program at a for-profit college experienced lower returns on their investment in education compared with students who completed an associate's degree program at a

224 Ibid.

225 Ibid., 16.

226 Ibid.

227 Kevin Lang and Russell Weinstein, "Evaluating Student Outcomes at For-Profit Colleges," National Bureau of Economic Research Working Paper 18201, June 2012, 25.

public college.[228] Overall, students from for-profit colleges have worse labor market outcomes in terms of earnings and employment rates compared with students who attend public colleges. Yet that is where the managers of USA Inc. most aggressively increased the rate of taxpayer support, while cutting support for the better-performing nonprofit institutions. While it is possible that the managers of USA Inc. are just really bad at spending taxpayer dollars, it would also be interesting to see the levels and changes in campaign contributions and lobbying by for-profit institutions. It would not be surprising to see a significant and increasing amount spent on campaign contributions and lobbying, because, as we saw, not much seems to be spent on the students.

While for-profit colleges have tuition rates that are significantly higher than public colleges, for-profits spend less per student on education-related expenses that improve the quality of education. And even though short, occupation-specific certificate programs at for-profits produce better outcomes than associate's and bachelor's degree programs at for-profits, they are still not a good investment for students and taxpayers of USA Inc. These short certificate

Overall, students from for-profit colleges have worse labor market outcomes in terms of earnings and employment rates compared with students who attend public colleges. Yet that is where the managers of USA Inc. most aggressively increased the rate of taxpayer support, while cutting support for the better performing nonprofit institutions.

228 Ibid.

programs at for-profit colleges do not provide better outcomes than similar certificate programs at community colleges, but they cost significantly more.

For-profit colleges are more expensive across all degree and certificate programs than public colleges, have lower retention rates than public colleges, lower success rates than public colleges in terms of unemployment rates and wage rates, and spend less per student per year on education-related expenses that improve the educational quality of their programs. Despite short, occupation-specific programs at for-profit colleges faring better than their associate's and bachelor's degree programs, they are still a poor investment for students and taxpayers of USA Inc. These short certificate programs do not provide better outcomes than similar certificate programs at community colleges and cost an average of four times as much. These facts lead to obvious solutions.

It is imperative that USA Inc. invest more in community college programs and less in for-profit programs. Congress should be investing more dollars where the odds of increasing the human capital utilization rate and productivity of USA Inc.'s labor force is the greatest, not where it is least, as they have been. We can do better.

It is imperative that USA Inc. invest more in community college programs and less in for-profit programs. Congress should be investing more dollars where the odds of increasing the human capital utilization rate and productivity of USA Inc.'s labor force is the greatest, not where it is least, as they have been. We can do better.

This begins with ending the trend of decreasing

state support for public colleges and increasing tuition rates for public colleges. We saw earlier that state funding for public two-year community colleges and four-year colleges in the 2017 school year was nearly $9 billion below its 2008 level, after adjusting for inflation. This decrease in funding has contributed to raising tuition, reducing faculty, limiting course offerings, and in some cases, closing campuses. As states have decreased higher education funding, the price of attending a public college has risen significantly faster than what families can afford. For the average student, increases in federal student aid and the availability of tax credits have not kept up, jeopardizing the ability of many to afford the college education that is necessary for their success in the labor market. To increase the human capital utilization rate of USA Inc., states need to increase financial support for public colleges, the very institutions providing the highest return on investment for students—and, therefore, for USA Inc., because today's students are the future workers of USA Inc.

Achieving a better return on USA Inc.'s investment in post-secondary education requires additional solutions.

Expanding the Middle Class Solution #4: Taxpayer funding going to for-profit colleges is subject to meeting rigorous ROI evaluation concerning whether students complete the program and earn high enough wages to justify the investment and pay back their student loans.

Expanding the Middle Class Solution #5: Ensure that potential students can view the costs and expected benefits from a program in a simple and standardized format, allowing them to make better and more informed decisions

Expanding the Middle Class Solution #6: Counseling by an independent third party that helps students understand the financial aid packages and student loan obligations can potentially decrease the very high loan default rate for students at for-profit colleges.

SECTION V

INCREASING CONGRESSIONAL TRANSPARENCY AND ACCOUNTABILITY

33. TOWARD A MORE RESPONSIVE CONGRESS

Implementing the solutions contained in the previous pages is contingent on Congress. Why? Because management implements, and Congress is USA Inc.'s management. Just as getting management to implement company policies requires knowing what management is doing and holding them accountable when they don't, getting Congress to implement the solutions will require greater congressional transparency and accountability. I know, easier said than done…but it can and must be done.

The reality is that Congress sometimes represents very small but powerful special interests as opposed to the greater interest of USA Inc., meaning we need a series of solutions to make Congress more responsive and accountable to the shareholders of USA Inc. Notice that I am neither blaming nor expecting unions, corporations, lobbyists, or CEOs to implement these solutions. Why not?

We didn't vote for them. We did vote for members of Congress. As the shareholders of USA Inc., we are justified in expecting that members of Congress would implement the desires or, in this case, the solutions put forth by its shareholders. Let me give you an example illustrating why it is Congress, first and foremost, that is at fault for USA Inc.'s missed opportunities.

One year after the financial collapse of Lehman Brothers, Congress summoned the CEOs of the largest banks and Wall Street firms to Washington, D.C., for a very public media flogging. The proceedings were filled with members of Congress expressing varying forms of outrage and indignation at the actions of the financial institutions each CEO represented. However, the displays of outrage and indignation rang hollow. They came across as disingenuous and self-serving. It, sadly, was just another self-centered endeavor, with hopes of making themselves appear just as outraged as the country. They knew the country was outraged and expected the same outrage from their congressmen. Their actions appeared more sanctimonious than sincere because for all their condemnation of the financial institutions' actions, not a single member of Congress was able to say that any of it was illegal. Congress was berating the CEOs and their institutions for actions that *Congress* gave their legislative blessing to. President Trump's former top economic advisor, Gary Cohn, indirectly made this point on the ten-year anniversary of the Great Financial Crisis, stating, "Who broke the law? I just want to know who you think broke the law?"[229] This is the critical point:

229 Anna Irrera and Svea Herbst-Bayliss, "'Who Broke the Law?' Cohn Says in Defending Wall Street's Role in Crisis," Reuters, Sept. 17, 2018.

Everything that the bank CEOs were cited for during the hearings, Congress had sanctioned. The very actions the congressmen raged against were endorsed by Congress and made legal through congressional legislation. That is one example of why the road to implementing these solutions for improving our economic and political systems begins at 1st St. NE, Washington, D.C. 20001—the United States Capitol. While it doesn't end there, it certainly begins there.

The second reason we need a more transparent and accountable Congress is straightforward: Congressional action impacts broad swaths of the U.S.economy, and as a result, the individual finances of its shareholders. Congress makes laws, including corporate and personal income tax laws. It determines how the trillions of dollars of tax revenue, your money, is spent. It puts in place laws that lead to regulations that impact a wide range of industries and jobs. Congress has a significant impact on the economy, and as a result, USA Inc. and its shareholders.

Everything that the bank CEOs were cited for during the hearings, Congress had sanctioned. The very actions the congressmen raged against were endorsed by Congress and made legal through congressional legislation.

Think I am overstating the role Congress has played in USA Inc. falling short of its economic potential? Whether you believe corporations aren't paying their fair share in taxes or, conversely, if you think they are paying too much in taxes, remember that Congress made it possible. If you think companies shouldn't be able to reduce their taxes by the amount they spend closing manufacturing plants in the U.S., don't get mad at the companies. Get mad at Congress. If you think unions have too much or too little power, don't overlook Congress. Whether you think we have too much or too little financial regulation, remember, Congress is responsible. If you believe patent laws are restricting innovation, or perhaps you think patent laws aren't robust enough, know that Congress dictates the patent laws. Congress plays a major role in our economy. That, along with the fact that we vote for members of Congress, is why we need an entire section containing solutions for creating a more transparent, accountable, and responsive Congress.

34. THE INHERENT CHALLENGE IN REPRESENTATIVE GOVERNMENT: THE PRINCIPAL-AGENT PROBLEM

> *The very principle that We the People rely on for governance, representative government, is a key source of our problems in Congress.*

The very principle that We the People rely on for governance, representative government, is a key source of our problems in Congress. A more responsive Congress begins with understanding that, like our banking system, Congress has a principal-agent problem. As it relates to Congress, we are the principals, and members of Congress are our agents, theoretically acting on our behalf. Not surprisingly, conflicts of interest abound in Congress, exacerbated by the Supreme Court of the United States ensuring continued flows of massive amounts of money into politics. As a result, sometimes some members of Congress are more focused on their interests and the special interests of those with disproportionate financial influence over them than the interests of We the People.

The $156 Billion Congressional Principal-Agent Problem

Just how big of a problem can the principal-agent problem cause? One former member of Congress secured tens of billions of dollars in benefits for the pharmaceutical industry at a cost to the shareholders of USA Inc. of $156 billion.[230] What did the former congressman subsequently do? He secured employment with a pharmaceutical trade association, making $2 million a year.[231] Meet former Congressman Billy Tauzin (D-La.), one example of the principal-agent problem in Congress. Don't recognize the name? That is part of the problem, not enough transparency; more on that later.

We the People fund Medicare Part D through our taxes, and the U.S. government is the largest single buyer of pharmaceuticals, a position that should give the U.S. government substantial bargaining power that results in highly favorable pricing on pharmaceuticals it purchases. Yet in 2003, the pharmaceutical industry successfully lobbied to restrict the government's ability to negotiate lower drug prices in Medicare Part D, costing U.S. taxpayers an estimated $156 billion. Who were the key players in placing this restriction on the government? The Pharmaceutical Research and Manufacturers of America's congressional cheerleader, former Congressman Tauzin. According to CBS' *60 Minutes*, Tauzinwas responsible for successfully shepherding a bill through Congress in 2003 that prevented the government from leveraging its purchasing power to negotiate better drug prices. According to the health care consumer advocacy group Families USA, this resulted in Medicare

230 "Tax Payers in America Are Overpaying Billions of Dollars for Medicare & Medicaid Drugs," TheMedicareCoach.com, July 6, 2016.

231 Tom Hamburger, "Drug Industry Lobbyist Billy Tauzin to Resign," *Los Angeles Times*, Feb. 12, 2010.

paying far more for its drugs than the Department of Veterans Affairs. It has been estimated that Medicare pays from 40 percent to 58 percent[232] more for its pharmaceuticals on average than Veterans Affairs—quite a "win" for the pharmaceutical industry and a loss for We the People. The former congressman was well-rewarded, retiring sometime after securing the favorable restriction and accepting a position as president of a trade association at $2 million a year. Which one? Surprise, surprise, the Pharmaceutical Research and Manufacturers of America. But that wasn't all the former congressman reaped. In 2011, the year after being involved in passage of President Obama's Affordable Care Act (ACA), Tauzin was the highest-paid health care lobbyist, garnering a staggering $11.6 million.[233]

Some have tried to argue that the prohibition placed on the government against negotiating better prices is not the cause for the difference in prices between Veterans Affairs drug costs and Medicare drug costs. First, if that is the case, why did the pharmaceutical industry insert it into the bill? Second, it flies in the face of the merits of the free market to posit that this restriction on the free market had no impact on pricing. Finally, if this restriction was inconsequential, would they be willing to take this restriction out?

---

232 Walid F. Gellad, Sebastian Schneeweiss, Phyllis Brawarsky, Stuart Lipsitz, and Jennifer S. Haas, "What if The Federal Government Negotiated Prices for Seniors? An Estimate of National Savings," *Journal of General Internal Medicine* 23, no. 9 (June 26, 2008); and Michael Hiltzik, "Why Big Pharma's Patient-Assistance Programs Are a Sham," *Los Angeles Times*, Sept. 25, 2015.

233 Alex Wayne and Drew Armstrong, "Tauzin's $11.6 Million Made Him Highest-Paid Health-Law Lobbyist," Bloomberg, Nov. 29, 2011.

We already know the answer to this last question. We will see later that that the pharmaceutical industry has fought tooth and nail to preserve this provision, spending tens of millions on lobbying.

How could removing this provision save U.S. taxpayers so much money—bargaining power? Medicare Part D provided benefits for 41 million Americans in 2015, and recipients are estimated to increase to 57 million by 2025—that's a lot of customers.[234] Just how much did the government spend to provide pharmaceutical benefits for those 41 million—$62 billion...in one year?[235] This is estimated to increase to an average of $111 billion per year over the next decade.[236] Now, that's bargaining power, and that is part of how Congress could save the American taxpayer billions...if it wanted to.

Why wasn't this massive buying power used for the benefit of U.S. taxpayers? Because we live under a system of lobbyism that is distorting the free market and capitalism. How powerful is our system of lobbyism? In 2011, the year Congressman Peter Welch (D-Vt.) tried to remove the restriction on negotiating drug prices, the Pharmaceutical Research and Manufacturers of America spent nearly $19 million lobbying Congress, while pharmaceutical manufacturers spent another $130 million. The nine most aggressive pharmaceutical companies alone spent more than $67 million. They undoubtedly sell some drugs to Medicare. These nine multinationals alone comprised more than 50 percent of the lobbying

---

234 "Fact Sheet: How Much Money Could Medicare Save by Negotiating Prescription Drug Prices?" Committee for a Responsible Federal Budget, April 11, 2016.

235 Ibid.

236 Ibid.

dollars spent by pharmaceutical manufacturers in 2011.[237] Consider the return on "investment"—$67 *million* spent on lobbying to make $156 *billion* over the next ten years? Now that's an impressive ROI. Talk about a principal-agent problem. Talk about a misalignment of interests.

> We live under a system of lobbyism that is distorting the free market and capitalism.

They're Baaack!

Have you heard the phrase "made man"? In the Mafia, it means you are untouchable. Incumbent members of Congress are similarly untouchable: 98 percent of House incumbents and 93 percent of Senate[238] incumbents were reelected in 2016. They very nearly have the equivalent of tenure in the education field; ironically, that's something some members of Congress rail against.

Absent lucrative post-congressional opportunities, why would members want to leave once they are ensconced in Congress? Members have subsidized health care, while our veterans wait in line in hopes of someday maybe receiving health care—health care of a quality that no member of Congress would ever stand for. Members' pensions

> 98 percent of House incumbents and 93 percent of Senate incumbents were reelected in 2016.

237 "Pharmaceuticals/Health Products, Industry Profile: Summary, 2011," OpenSecrets.org.

238 Kyle Kondik and Geoffrey Skelley, "Incumbent Reelection Rates Higher Than Average in 2016," *Rasmussen Reports,* Dec. 15, 2016.

are exempt from the cuts facing many public pensioners, and they get to determine how big their pay raises are. As it relates to laws, they have it even better than the Mob: They not only make the laws, they literally live above the laws, exempting themselves from the laws they impose on us. Remember when Congress exempted itself from insider trading laws, making it legal for them to trade on non-public information? Trading stocks on insider information is illegal for you and me, but it wasn't for members of Congress. It was like they could go to the horse track and be privately told that the horse favored to win the race was injured, while the rest of us chumps bet on the favorite.

In a hopeful sign that shows the power of public scrutiny, when the exemption was made public and public pressure became too great, Congress eliminated the exemption.

98 percent of House incumbents and 93 percent of Senate incumbents were reelected in 2016.

35. THE FOUR-STEP CONGRESSIONAL RECOVERY PLAN

So what to do? You've heard of the Texas two-step? Well, for Congress we need a four-step recovery plan, because two just won't do it. Congress and its members, also known as the managers of USA Inc., need to go through a four-step recovery process:

1. Start Attracting a Different Type of Member to Congress
2. Transparency: Congress Comes Out of the Shadows
3. Accountability: Make Getting "Pinched" a Credible Threat
4. Minimize Influence of Campaign Donations

Step 1—Start Attracting a Different Type of Member to Congress

Of Glory Hounds, Power Addicts, Financial Opportunists, and Political Party Pawns

While some go to Congress with good intentions trying to pursue the interests of We the People, it is safe to say that there are also bad apples in Congress. They include Glory Hounds, basking in the limelight of their office; Power Addicts, addicted to the power that comes with overseeing trillions of dollars of spending and regulatory powers; Financial Opportunists, angling for their golden parachute after their time in Congress; and Party Pawns, those without any expertise or drive beyond doing the bidding of the political parties that put them in office and keep them there. They are all manifestations of the principal-agent problem.

The principal problem with some in Congress is that they are representing everyone except We the People. They can spend more time at fundraising events than on the events and issues impacting We the People. Having collected their checks, they then do the bidding of the highest bidders from the fundraising events. Members of Congress can be influenced by a few donors exerting disproportionate financial influence. While it may be representative government, it does not include equal representation in government.

> While it may be representative government, it does not include equal representation in government.

USA Inc. has experienced a not-so-hostile takeover by big *donors.* We have our Supreme Court to thank for making it all possible. It is no longer government of the people, by the people, and for the people. Rather, we have a 3-D government: government of the largest *donors,* by the largest donors, and for the largest *donors.*

> We have a 3-D government: government of the largest *donors,* by the largest *donors,* and for the largest *donors.*

Take Away the Sugar

Now, what would a business owner do if he or she realized they weren't attracting the type of employees they were looking for? First, they would take away what is attracting the bad apples. For Congress, that means making Congress less cushy. Just how cushy is Congress? Congress has perks that would make CEOs blush. They determine their own pay increases, pensions are sacred, they receive subsidized health care, and it is the only place in America where, at times, it has been legally okay to trade stocks on insider information.

Next, good managers understand the needs and pains of their customers. Better yet, they have experienced the same needs and pains. Given their near-guaranteed job status, ability to raise their own salaries, and sacrosanct pensions, it is unrealistic to think that the pain of declining middle-skill jobs, disappointing wage growth, and pension cuts are at the top of every member's concerns. And forget about concern over bad schools. How many members of Congress or their children have spent time in public schools? It is time Congress' interest was tied more closely to ours. It is time they felt our pains. It is time they lived in the same world we do. Their experience in Congress needs to become a little less cushy.

Members of Congress Go to the Back of the VA Health Care Line and to the Front Lines of Our Public Schools

How do we start making members of Congress feel their constituents' pain? In honor of my uncles and all veterans, I am going to start with our veterans and Veterans Affairs. Veterans wait fifty-one days on average and up to seventy days to see a physician[239] When they do receive services, they can be so substandard that no member of Congress would stand for it. My Uncle Peter used to lie in bed in a VA hospital calling out for help, with no response. Unfortunately, veterans still suffer from not only substandard care, but also even harmful care. A March 29, 2019 USA Today story reported on the results of surprise inspections conducted at VA nursing homes. 28 facilities were cited for "failing to ensure veterans didn't suffer from serious pain. 52 out of the 99 facilities across 25 states had deficiencies that caused harm to veterans. The inspections also sadly revealed that veterans in 50 of the nursing homes were exposed to hazardous conditions." It would not be surprising to hear of similar and worse stories from readers. And members of Congress, if they had an interest, should have known about this for years. The same USA Today story reported that more than seven years ago, the General Accountability Office documented a high percentage of veterans were in pain. It is time members of Congress had the same health care experience as our veterans. It is time they go to the back of the VA line, see how long it takes to receive services, and experience firsthand the low quality of services some veterans are receiving. It is shameful that veterans serve the country and

239 Leo Shane III, "Report: Vets Still Face Long Waits With VA Choice Program," *Military Times*, June 4, 2018

then wait nearly two months on average just to see a doctor or else suffer in pain and are exposed to harmful conditions in VA nursing facilities.

Congressional Solution #1: Require members of Congress to receive their health care from the lowest-rated VA hospital located in their district or state and go to the back of the queue of veterans waiting for services.

Our education system offers another opportunity make Congress less cushy and make its members feel our pain. The poor state of our public schools is a national economic emergency. Our children are not the only casualty of our nation's deficient public-school system. The economy is harmed. How do we expect the economy to increase its productivity, expand, and provide a highly employable workforce with subpar public schools? We shouldn't. How best to get members of Congress to work harder on our public schools' crisis?

Congressional Solution #2: Require members of Congress to serve as teacher's aides one month of every year they are in office, in the lowest-achieving school in their district or state. Here is the irony: It wouldn't be surprising if they were the first teacher's aide the school had in years due to limited school funding.

Some may say education shouldn't be included here because the federal government funds such a small portion of education. The federal government still provides substantial funds through the Department of Education, spending billions of dollars on education. If our managers are investing that much money in education, they should have firsthand experience with how our tax dollars are being spent. No more of this absentee approach to management of our tax dollars. Second, our education system is a national emergency with direct implications for whether USA Inc. moves closer to achieving its economic potential. Having to work in the worst-performing school in their district or state will also make those expecting a cushy job in Congress think twice.

Congress Has a Truancy Problem

Congress has an absenteeism problem. First, members work a Tuesday-through-Thursday legislative schedule. Second, according to the Government Printing Office, which maintains congressional calendars, in 2016 the House was in session 131 days and the Senate 165 days—that is less than half the year! Most Americans would love that. Americans working five days a week are at work 240 days a year, even after accounting for two weeks'vacation and ten federal holidays. Even when members are in session, some members have a habit of skipping out on work, including congressional hearings. If you doubt this, watch a congressional hearing on C-Span. Some members come to a hearing only for their five minutes of questioning, and that is when there is the possibility of getting media coverage. Then they leave.

Considering the magnitude of issues facing our country, that is unacceptable. There is a solution for that.

<u>Congressional Solution #3</u>: Members of Congress shall only vote on bills if they attended the hearings pertaining to the bill… and more than five minutes of the hearings.

It is ridiculous to have members voting on bills when they skipped the hearings or only stayed for five minutes.

Congress Needs to Start Doing Its Homework

Then there is the issue of Congress not doing its homework. How many members of Congress read the bills they are voting on? My guess is probably not many. In their defense, how can they read the bills when they need to spend massive amounts of time fundraising? Thanks to the Supreme Court, members of Congress are more akin to professional fundraisers than legislators. That, however, does not excuse them from doing their jobs and knowing the content of the bills they are voting on. This will also go a long way in making the job less cushy.

Congressional Solution #4: Members of Congress shall be required to read a detailed summary of each bill they vote on and certify that they agree with the key provisions outlined in the summary. The summaries should be provided by a non-partisan source, much like the Congressional Budget Office provides independent budget and economic analysis.

Members of Congress are more akin to professional fundraisers than legislators.

Some may say that it is unrealistic for members of Congress to even read summaries of the bills they are voting on. Given how much time they have to spend fundraising, it may be challenging for them. But the answer isn't to exempt them from reading the bills, it is to reduce the amount of time they have to spend fundraising. In the interim, they should at least be required to read a detailed summary of each they vote on.

While these solutions would make the job less cushy, reduce truancy, and ensure members are familiar with the most important provisions of the bills they are voting on, members also have a problem with making laws and then exempting themselves from the laws. This leads to our next solution:

Congressional Solution #5: Congress shall exempt itself from no law passed and imposed on We the People.

We shouldn't have to state this, but given what has happened, it is necessary. All you have to do is be reminded of how Congress exempted itself from the insider trading laws we all have to live under.

Members of Congress Start Living in the Same Economic Climate as Those They Are Supposed to Represent

Since the 1970s, middle-income wages have been flat when accounting for inflation.[240] The bottom tenth saw a meager 3 percent cumulative increase in inflation-adjusted weekly earnings from 2000 to 2018.[241] Congress, however, determines its own pay raises. But it gets even better for members of Congress. They legislated themselves automatic pay raises. Members don't even have to vote for them. To their credit, they voted to not receive the automatic pay raises since 2010. Despite this, since 2000, congressional salaries still increased from $141,000 to $174,000.[242] Can members of Congress be motivated to work on increasing the average American's pay when they can simply increase their own salaries? Let's at

240 Drew DeSilver, "For Most U.S. workers, Real Wages Have Barely Budged in Decades," Pew Research Center, Aug. 7, 2018.

241 Ibid.

242 "About Member of Congress Salaries," Legistorm, https://www.legistorm.com/member_of_congress_salaries.html.

least ensure they feel the economic pain of those experiencing the slowest growth in pay.

Congressional Solution #6: Base congressional salary increases on the rate of increase in the bottom tenth's inflation-adjusted weekly earnings.

Under this solution, if the lowest tenth doesn't see wage increases, members' wages don't either. Why is this so critical? Because approximately 70 percent of GDP is driven by consumer spending. It is time Congress has an incentive to focus on what drives the largest component of GDP growth—consumer earnings.

Congress Goes From Unreal Retirements to the Very Real Retirement Insecurity Many Have to Face

It is time Congress has an incentive to focus on what drives the largest component of GDP growth—consumer earnings.

Members of Congress have untouchable pensions, pensions that most would love to have. Yet pensions of the firemen and policemen across the country that protect us are at risk of being cut. Whether you agree or disagree with public employee pension cuts, if public service employees are being asked to take pension cuts, why not members of Congress? How can they take the issue of unfunded pensions seriously when their pensions are not at risk?

Congressional Solution #7: Cut congressional pensions when public-sector pensions are cut, and in the same proportions.

Continuing with the retirement theme, every now and again, there is talk of cutting Social Security. What if Social Security gets cut? Should congressional pensions remain sacrosanct? Of course not.

Congressional Solution #8: Congressional pensions are cut when cuts are made to Social Security, and in the same proportion.

Every so often, there is also talk of applying means-testing to Social Security. The general idea is that those with greater financial means would receive less in Social Security payments and maybe no payments compared to those of lesser financial means. Financial factors such as savings, net worth, amount of pensions received, and other factors can be used to evaluate the financial means of individuals. Whether or not you agree with the idea of means-testing Social Security, one thing is for sure: If Congress implements means-testing of Social Security for We the People, then their Social Security should certainly be means-tested as well. This is important, since nearly 47 percent or 203 members of Congress are millionaires.[243]

Congressional Solution #9: If means testing for Social Security payments is implemented, members of Congress should also have their Social Security payments means tested, and the factors used to evaluate their financial means should include their Congressional pensions and government-subsidized healthcare, among other factors.

Now let's deal with the ultimate financial opportunists, those who see Congress as a cushy stepping-stone to a highly paid post-Congress job. While tying congressional pensions to public employee pensions and Social Security is critical to getting Congress

243 Randy Leonard, "Every Member of Congress' Wealth in One Chart," *Roll Call*, March 2, 2018.

interested in the subject of pensions and Social Security, the most lucrative financial opportunities come after their time in Congress before retirement. If we are to stop attracting financial opportunists, the revolving door from Congress to ludicrous lobbyist paydays must finally be ended.

"Casino Jack" Abramoff on Congressional Staffers—"I Owned Them"

Remember former lobbyist James "Casino Jack" Abramoff? He went to jail for engaging in illegal lobbying practices. He was interviewed on December 6, 2014, by Lawrence Lessig at Harvard's Edmond J. Safra Center for Ethics. Now, you may rightfully ask, "Why was James Abramoff, of all people, speaking at the Harvard Center for Ethics?" He was speaking there because it was the equivalent of having a world-class thief telling you how he successfully robbed banks and art museums. In this case, Abramoff described how he manipulated the American political system and got what he wanted for his clients—all for a handsome fee, of course. What was most instructive was his answer to the following question: How did you get members of Congress in your pocket? First, he said that he focused less on the members of Congress and more on the staffers, because they had more influence in the process. Abramoff said he "owned" the staffers. To get them, he would dangle the prospect of working for him. Paraphrasing him: "Once they knew there was the possibility of lucrative employment after Congress, I owned them."

"Once they knew there was the possibility of lucrative employment after Congress, I owned them."

Abramoff went on to say that they were actually more valuable to him than his own employees, because the staffers were still in the system and knew the critical developments and interactions occurring on the Hill on a daily basis. These revelations lead to our next congressional solution:

Congressional Solution #10: Prohibit members of Congress and staffers from working as lobbyists for the greater of five years or half the number of years they were members or congressional staffers.

Now, some may say this would restrict their right to work. Really? They can fend for themselves in the private market like We the People. It is not uncommon as a condition of employment for companies to impose non-compete agreements, which prohibit employees from working for competing firms in the future. Members of Congress and congressional staffers should not be allowed to profit from the influence they have over the congressional system at our expense. Additionally, this removes one of the key tools that lobbyists use to influence members of Congress and their staffs—the promise of future employment. As we saw with the principal-agent problem, we need to limit the misalignment of interests between members of Congress and We the People.

Subject Congress to a Fiduciary Standard of Conduct

The Supreme Court's rulings on campaign finance laws make it tempting for members of Congress to act in the interest of a few large donors, as opposed to the interest of the majority that elected them. This can be addressed by introducing a fiduciary level standard of conduct for members of Congress and congressional staffers. Corporations have standards of conduct for employees. They put employees through extensive training surrounding their standards of conduct. We need a very specific standard for Congress, a fiduciary standard. What is a fiduciary duty? From the Cornell University law school website: "A fiduciary duty is a legal duty to act solely in another party's interests."

Congressional Solution #11: Members of Congress shall be held to a legal standard of a fiduciary, having a legal duty to act solely in the interest of all the people they represent, not just a few, and certainly not themselves.

Step 2—Transparency: It's Time Congress Came Out of the Shadows

Taking a Page From the Feds

Implementing a fiduciary standard is a necessary step. However, it won't change anything if we don't know how members of Congress are spending their time. It is like telling a crime syndicate that they can't rob banks and then not tracking their activities. We need to track the behavior of our management—a.k.a. Congress. We need far greater transparency. It is time to start monitoring more closely the activities of members of Congress. Smoke-filled back rooms have merely been replaced with smoke-free back rooms, texting, emails, and cell phone conversations, among other means of communications, the contents of which we know nothing.

> It is like telling a crime syndicate that they can't rob banks and then not tracking their activities.

Congress is filled with individuals who are experts at keeping track of their time—lawyers. Why aren't members of Congress required to keep track of how they spend their time like private-sector lawyers do? We the People could see who spent the most time on the campaign trail and at fundraising events versus the time they spent in the office. This would promote transparency as well as allowing members of Congress to be compared against each other—we could rank them! Nothing like a little competition. You would hope that nobody would want to be the member who spent the most time at campaign fundraisers.

This solution would create the Observer or Hawthorne Effect. This is a change in behavior that occurs when an individual knows they are being watched. Think of it like having a teacher looking over your shoulder when you were in elementary school. If members of Congress still get "recesses," then clearly, they need someone looking over their shoulder.

Congressional Solution #12: Require members of Congress to track the time they spend on campaign-related matters, including but not limited to fundraising, campaign events, and travel time.

Congressional Solution #13: Develop and implement a searchable online database that allows We the People to monitor how much time members of Congress are spending on campaign-related matters.

Now that we have the data, it's time we take a page from online price comparison websites.

Congressional Solution #14: Create and implement an online comparison tool, complete with scorecards for each member of Congress, ranking them against their fellow members in time spent on campaign-related matters.

Why don't we know how much time members of Congress actually spend in their office, offices of the fellow members of Congress, and at the Capitol? With today's technology, that can easily be fixed.

Congressional Solution #15: Install biometric sensors that members of Congress use to enter and exit their offices, the various committee conference rooms, various member office buildings, and the House or Senate chamber.

As they are the servants on the payroll of the taxpayers, we deserve to know how they are spending their time and how much time they are spending "in the office."

But that's just scratching the surface of the level of transparency we need. Doubt this? The more the Supreme Court allows unlimited and anonymous campaign donations, the more we need to know how members are spending their time, with whom, and what is being communicated. Employers have the right to read employee emails and listen to their phone calls. Why don't we have the right to read the work-related emails and listen to the work-related phone calls of those supposedly working for us? The last time I checked, members of Congress were employed *and* paid by us, We the People, regardless of how many $20 million individual donations they receive. Hackers shouldn't be the only ones able to read the work-related emails of members of Congress.

Congressional Solution #16: Record, store, and provide online access, in a searchable format, to every congressional member's work email. Congressional staffers' work-related accounts too. They should have nothing to hide.

Hackers shouldn't be the only ones able to read the work-related emails of members of Congress.

We also need to know what is being communicated via telephone.

Congressional Solution #17: Record, store, and provide online access, in a searchable format, to every congressional member's and staffer's phone system.

It is time we utilized technology to address one of the key elements of the principal-agent problem, not knowing what your agent is doing.

Anticipating the objection to these solutions based on members of Congress dealing with sensitive national security matters, the solutions would include exemptions for content in emails and telephone calls that require security clearance.

There is another transparency issue we need to address—campaign contributions. There are some organizations that have done a lot to make donor information available online. But why not make it even easier? Why not allow We the People to literally see who the donors are? This leads to the last transparency solution, a solution I know others have proposed.

Congressional Solution #18: Members of Congress wear NASCAR-type suits of their sponsors, otherwise known as largest campaign donors, with logos proudly displayed.

For those who might scoff at this solution, if a picture is worth a thousand words, then having logos of the largest donors on the suits of members of Congress should be priceless. Well, actually not priceless—it just depends on how many millions the donor is willing to pay to influence the member. Besides, if our Supreme Court has placed free speech through campaign donations on such sacred ground, why would we prohibit the largest donors from being able to publicly express their undying support for their most valued members of Congress?

Step 3—Accountability: It's Time More Members of Congress Get "Pinched"

Implementing the steps previously outlined would change the type of members we are attracting to Congress and increase congressional transparency, the first steps in making Congress more responsive. The next step is to weed out those already in Congress who do not fit the profile We the People are looking for. However, as we saw, in the list of life's certainties, getting re-elected to the House of Representatives isn't far behind death and taxes. Many members of Congress have a form of tenure, a nearly permanent status as a member of Congress. Some may say, "They can be voted out of office." In theory, yes. Yet it rarely happens. How rare is it? From 1960 to 2018, the average reelection rate of incumbent members of the House of Representatives was nearly 93 percent[244]—talk about a sure thing. This is critical because, even if the transparency solutions were adopted and members of Congress knew they were being watched more closely, if there isn't a credible threat of being voted out of office, the impact of the solutions is muted. If there is no accountability, there is no incentive to change. Think of it this way: If someone is caught stealing or selling drugs but there are no negative consequences, why would he stop? It seems that, in the case of the bad apples in Congress, most Americans think they haven't stopped. A December 2018 Gallup poll showed that 18 percent of Americans approved of Congress. Yet the re-election rate is above 90 percent. How do we increase the connection between

244 Tom Murse, "Do Members of Congress Ever Lose Reelection?" ThoughtCo.com, Jan. 24, 2018.

disapproval and, as the Mob would say, members getting "pinched?" Let's start with the first source of disconnect, gerrymandering.

Gerrymandering—Sowing Political Stagnation, Low Voter Turnout, and Extremism

The disconnect between voter disgust with Congress and the sky-high re-election rates of members of the House of Representatives is at least partially due to the undemocratically high number of "safe" seats. The October 2018 *The Cook Political Report* rated more than 75 percent of House of Representative seats as solidly Republican or Democrat, otherwise known as "safe" seats, making it very difficult for the other party to beat the candidate from the advantaged party. What percentage of seats did *The Cook Report* rate as a toss-up? Just over 10 percent. Why is this?

Gerrymandering is when one political party draws voting district boundaries that ensures it has an advantage in elections. The goal of gerrymandering is to distort political representation. The party drawing the maps has disproportionate political influence. It is undemocratic, providing a political advantage to one party at the expense of an opposing group of voters. Gerrymandering rigs the political game to benefit one political party over another at the expense of voters.

> Gerrymandering rigs the political game to benefit one political party over another at the expense of voters.

Gerrymandering involves "packing" and "cracking." Packing is drawing voting boundaries to concentrate voters of the opposing party into as few districts as possible. limiting their number of seats. Conversely, cracking is drawing district maps to disperse voters of the opposing party across as many districts as possible. This reduces their influence on election outcomes. The goal is to create as many favorable districts as possible while minimizing the number of the opposing party's favorable districts. Small wonder so many seats are rated as "safe." We the People get political stagnation, much like stagnant water in a swamp.

Gerrymandering and the related outcome of so many seats being safe result in low voter turnout, contributing to high re-election rates. Low voter turnout is not a new problem. Prior to the 2018 midterm elections, the last time voter turnout was even above 45 percent was 1968.[245] More recently, voter turnout dipped in 2014 to 36.7 percent.[246] That means that, in 2014, barely more than one in three of the eligible American electorate determined who was going to spend trillions of our tax dollars and make the laws that impact everything from our water, air pollution, food, and a myriad of businesses.

Low voter turnout is not a new problem. Prior to the 2018 midterm elections, the last time voter turnout was even above 45 percent was 1968.

How big of an impact does gerrymandering and its outcome of limited competitive districts have on voter turnout? A 2017 paper by Joel Jordan of Western Washington University, "The Effect of Electoral Competitiveness

245 Michael P. McDonald, "U.S. VEP Election Turnout 1789-Present: Statistics," United States Election Project, Feb. 20, 2019.

246 Ibid.

on Voter Turnout,"[247] concluded that uncontested congressional races had a 14.6 percent lower voter turnout rate. This is especially critical because it is likely the moderates who will stay home while the political zealots will still come out to vote, further increasing their influence beyond their numbers.

The result is generally candidates that appeal to the relatively small group of political zealots voting in primaries

Legislate reverse gerrymandering maximizing the number of competitive congressional districts and minimizing the number of safe districts.

Because of gerrymandering, low voter turnout and a primary system that is dominated by the more partisan elements of each party, election outcomes are often determined in the primary, not the general election. The result is generally candidates that appeal to the relatively small group of political zealots voting in primaries. This happens both on the left and the right. Then the winning candidates go to Washington, can't get anything done, and everyone looks around in disbelief as if this weren't predictable. Want to reduce political polarization and extremism? Legislate reverse gerrymandering, maximizing the number of competitive congressional districts and minimizing the number of safe districts.

247 Joel Jordan, "The Effect of Electoral Competitiveness on Voter Turnout" (Senior project, Western Washington University, 2017).

Congressional Solution #19: Implement reverse gerrymandering. Draw districts such that the greatest number of districts possible are evenly divided among registered voters of the Republican and Democratic parties.

This would make getting voted out of office a real threat, reducing the problem of congressional tenure. It would also lessen the presence of members with more partisan views and an intransigent attitude. The more partisan minority political bases would no longer wield more influence than the majority. This would allow for more moderate, pragmatic legislation, not ideologically driven impasses and extreme legislation. This would also help with the perception that America is extremely polarized. Part of the reason why the country seems so divided is because Congress is increasingly populated with more partisan members, enabled by gerrymandering. This is a critical problem as the best solutions are usually found in the middle, not at the extremes.

The best solutions are usually found in the middle, not at the extremes.

In order for reverse gerrymandering to work, we need higher voter participation rates. Those most likely to vote are referred to as the "base" of each party. They generally have all-or-nothing left- or right-leaning views. If the majority doesn't vote, small groups of dogmatic voters will continue determining elections. The most successful candidates will be the ones with more extreme positions. How can we increase voter participation rates? First, Jordan's paper documents the positive effect of mail-in ballots on voter participation rates. Jordan found that mail-in voting increased voter turnout by 7.7 percent—a meaningful rise. He further found that same-day voting also had a positive impact, increasing voter turnout by 5.8 percent. These are factors that can be controlled.

Congressional Solution #20: Implement mail-in voting in all congressional districts.

Congressional Solution #21: Implement same-day registration in all congressional districts.

In addition to the low voter turnout rates, there is a fascinating phenomenon that partially explains the disconnect between Congress' low voter approval ratings and the 90 percent-plus reelection rate among members of the House of Representatives.

Voters view every other member of Congress as a bum, but not their own representative. Why? It is easier to dislike someone you don't know rather than someone you know, even if only through campaign flyers, commercials, or news stories. It is easier to dislike an institution rather than someone you know and who is of your same party affiliation. All members of Congress may be bums, but not my member. As a result, members get re-elected at rates that do not reflect Congress' low approval rating.

Step 4 – Minimize the Influence of Campaign Donations

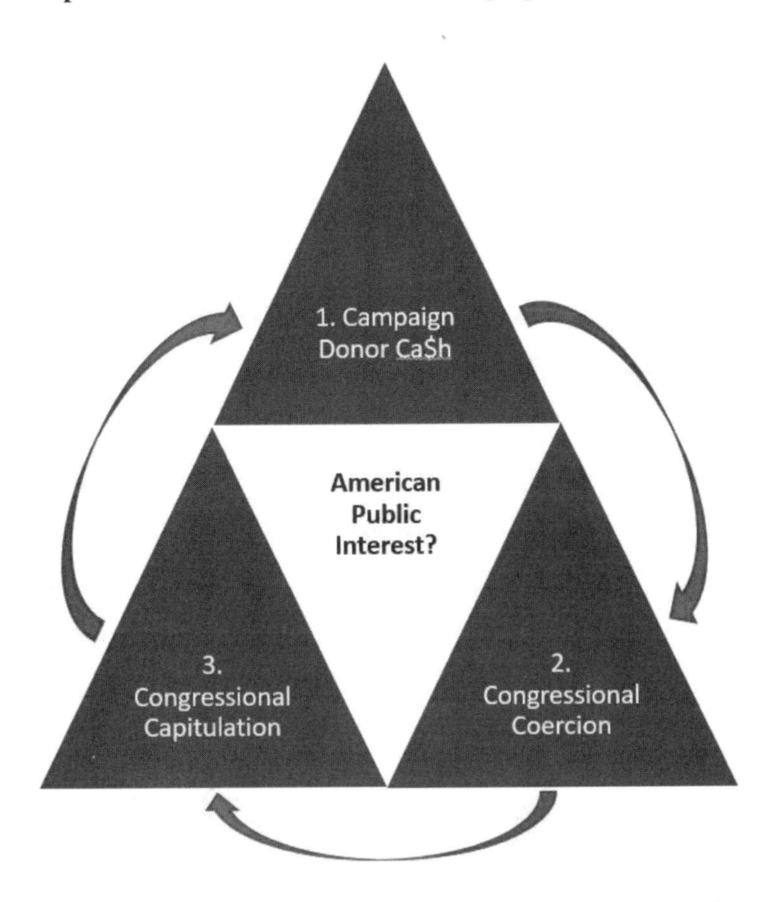

While it may be legal and called a campaign donation, when hundreds of thousands and even millions of dollars are given to elect members of Congress, it looks, at best, like an attempt to exert disproportionate influence and, at worse, a bribe. I'll let you decide what giving large sums of money to the campaigns of individuals running for Congress is. The following is the definition of a bribe from *The Merriam-Webster Dictionary*:

> *"1: money or favor given or promised in order to influence the judgment or conduct of a person in a position of trust. 2: something that serves to induce or influence.*

Regardless of what it is called and whether it is legal, giving inordinately large sums of money to influence election outcomes is a clear and present danger to our political system. It is an attempt to eliminate the spirit of equal representation and one person, one vote. It is an attempt to use disproportionate sums of money to achieve disproportionate political influence. The problem isn't special interests; everyone has their own special interests and the right to voice their interests. The problem is disproportionate influence by a few special interests.

> The problem isn't special interests; everyone has their own special interests and the right to voice their interests. The problem is disproportionate influence by a few special interests.

Campaign finance, enabled by our Supreme Court, has effectively turned the idea of one person, one vote, into an idealistic, naïve dream from a bygone era. Today's reality is much darker. Unlimited sums of money can be given to influence elections, anonymously, no less. Through what is called "Dark Money" pools, donors can anonymously give large sums of money to nonprofits engaging in political activities such as so-called issue ads. I say so-called because come on, who's kidding who? In reality these are often ads meant to influence the elections of individuals. Worse still, these organizations can give money to Super PACs, allowing Super PACs to get around the requirements for donor disclosure because they only have to disclose the Dark Money organization. That tells you nothing because contributions to these organizations can be anonymous.

How big of a role do these Dark Money organizations using anonymous donations play? These organizations spent more than $300 million during the 2012 presidential election cycle and $174 million during the 2014 midterm elections. Three of these groups alone, American Crossroads, Americans for Prosperity, and the U.S.Chamber of Commerce, have spent more than $140 million.[248] Three groups! When I talk about disproportionate influence of a few special interests, this is what I am referring to: large sums of anonymous money, spent by a few groups to influence elections. More recently, from January 1 through July 8, 2018, Dark Money organizations ran 47,000 television advertisements targeting Senate and House races, nearly 30,000 of which were from a mere five of these groups. Again, disproportionate influence by a few organizations and their secret donors.[249]

> If we can't limit the quantity of money, we need to focus on minimizing the effects of outsized campaign donations.

In Missouri, 42 percent of the dollars spent on the Senate race between incumbent Claire McCaskill and Republican Josh Hawley through July 8, 2018,

248 "2012 Outside Spending by Group," OpenSecrets.org.

249 Fredreka Schouten, "Election Ads Get Secret Funding," *The Arizona Republic*, July 13, 2018.

were from these types of Dark Money organizations, which are not required to disclose donor identities. And the role of Dark Money in Missouri is not the exception. In Wisconsin, Dark Money represented 46 percent of the spending in that state's U.S.Senate race.

What can we do about all this money creating outsized political influence? Well, the Supreme Court makes it difficult on us, as it seems to strike down most campaign finance laws. If we can't limit the quantity of money, we need to focus on minimizing the effects of outsized campaign donations.

Who Is It That I Need to Be Giving the Money To?

First, it is much more difficult to exert influence when you don't know who to influence. This leads to our first two campaign-donation-related solutions.

Congressional Solution #22: Randomly assign committee chairmanships and committee assignments.

Some may argue against this solution on the grounds that it deprives the shareholders of USA Inc. of the expertise built up by members serving on the same committees for years. Given the results we've had from Congress, I'm skeptical there is that much expertise. I'm willing to take the risk. Besides, a fresh set of eyes could be beneficial. The accounting industry learned this lesson. After a series of accounting scandals plagued the industry, it was decided that the auditing partner on an account is automatically rotated every five years. They were forced to rotate auditors to ensure that there was greater exposure and awareness of the activities of the companies being audited. Similarly, extra exposure and awareness of committee activities would be beneficial in Congress.

Randomizing committee assignments would also reduce the influence of the most powerful members of Congress. Under the current system, committee assignments are doled out in return for loyalty, a very concrete example of how a political party wields its influence to stifle independence and innovation. Either you support the senior party leaders, or you will be left off of key committees, limiting your ability to secure the "goodies" for your constituents.

Congressional Solution #23: Require campaign donations to be made before committee chairmanships and assignments are determined.

By requiring donations be made before committee assignments are determined, this eliminates the ability of donors to give large sums of cash to the election campaigns of those serving on committees impacting the donors' industries and businesses. If you don't know who the chairman or members of the congressional committees are that will be impacting your industry or business, you won't know who to give the bags of money to. Additionally, randomly assigning committee chairmanships and assignments will have the benefit of reducing the concentration of power among a few members of Congress. Today, party leaders wield great power through their ability to assign committee chairmanships and membership to highly desirable and influential congressional committees. As we saw, this creates a debt owed by those receiving the plum committee assignments. It is a debt which is used to require loyalty, restricting the ability of members to vote on bills based on merit, as opposed to the loyalty they owe to those wielding the power of committee assignments.

While wealthy donors might just give to all members of Congress and their PACs to ensure their bases are covered, there is a solution for that too:

Congressional Solution #24: If donors give money to members of Congress that are subsequently assigned to committees that impact the donor's industry or business, the member must return the money to the donor.

Those would somewhat help lessen the disproportionate influence of big money in campaigns.

Putting It All Together

These congressional solutions, if implemented, would go a long way in restoring the sense that Congress finally has some real oversight and accountability. They would also go a long way in attracting a different type of member of Congress. As a result, they would create confidence that we can do better. Voters need to have confidence that we can do better if they are going to participate in the political process. It becomes a self-fulfilling cycle as increased voter participation leads to better outcomes, which reinforces the belief that we can do better. As in any representative government, the effectiveness of the representatives and their adherence to constituent needs begin first with how broad the participation is among voters, because that determines whether small extremes or the majority controls the process.

The effectiveness of the representatives and their adherence to constituent needs begin first with how broad the participation is among voters, because that determines whether small extremes or the majority controls the process.

YOU'VE GOT THE POWER

My objective is that, after reading *Solutionomics*, you will see that there is a way to achieve America's economic potential, including higher wages and higher-paying jobs, greater financial security, increased company revenues, and reduced federal deficits. My hope is also that you will be spurred to enter the political process replacing your feelings of discouragement with engagement. Your participation is critical in transforming this potential into reality. You are the crucial ingredient. Through your actions, the solutions outlined will come to life. It is how we move from angst to action.

The first step is to increase awareness of the solutions. Awareness leads to action, which leads to change. Tell your friends, co-workers, and family about the solutions. Post your favorite solutions on your Facebook page, tweet them to your followers, and post them on Instagram. Call in to your favorite talk show and tell the host about a solution or ask the guest about a solution. Attend a town hall meeting, asking the elected official or candidate about the solutions. Awareness is the first step in adopting the solutions.

You are the crucial ingredient. Through your actions, the solutions outlined will come to life. It is how we move from angst to action.

Second, engage in the political process. Fortunately, the American voter has been roused from his slumber. She has been revived and energized, creating an electorate that has not been this animated in decades. After fifty years of hibernation, during which the median voter turnout during midterms was barely more than 39 percent, American voters awoke in 2018 and reengaged in the election process. Voters turned out in the 2018 midterm elections at a rate not seen since 1966 and nearly at a rate not seen during any election cycle since 1912.[250] How animated were voters? Nearly 50 percent[251] of eligible voters exercised their right to vote in 2018, up from a dismal 36.7 percent[252] in the last midterm election in 2014. While you may or may not agree with the results, in 2018, voters awoke and made a difference. To further put this in perspective, turnout in the 2018 midterm election was within five points of the turnout in the 1980 election that propelled Ronald Reagan to the White House and within three points of the 1996 election turnout that returned President Bill Clinton to the White House for another four years.[253] This is significant as midterm election turnout rates are typically well below presidential cycle election rates.

Just how big a difference did voters make in 2018? Twenty-one incumbent members of the House of Representatives lost[254]—a remarkable number considering how difficult it is to remove incumbents, especially congressional incumbents. Additionally, the last

250 "2018 November General Election Turnout Rates," United States Elections Project.

251 Ibid.

252 Ibid.

253 Ibid.

254 Alexi McCammond, "The Incumbents Who Lost in 2018," Axios, Nov. 8, 2018.

time Democrats gained more seats in the House of Representatives than in 2018 was over forty years ago in the Watergate-driven election of 1974.[255] On the other side of the aisle, in the Senate, voters penalized Democrats, sending three Democratic incumbents home.[256] At the state level, voters in eight states elected a governor from a different political party, a meaningful number especially when considering that two such changes involved incumbent governors.[257]

Despite America's recent history of low voter turnout, the 2018 midterms are not the only example of voters exercising their power to upend the establishment and political inertia to create change. Regardless of how you view the outcome, President Trump's election is the most recent proof that voters can make a difference and buck the establishment. Trump was the non-establishment candidate and was not only running against sixteen Republican establishment candidates in the primaries, he was running against the Republican Party itself. Beating sixteen establishment candidates and, in effect, the Republican Party is a powerful demonstration that voters can make a difference.

The election of former President Obama is another powerful example of the force that We the People can be when we set our minds to it. Again, whether you agree or disagree with the result, in 2008, the power of voters was enough to elect the country's first African-American President. Considering that, in the arc of history, it was not that long ago that schools were segregated, the election

255 Dan Balz and Michael Scherer, "For Democrats, a Midterm Election That Keeps on Giving," *The Washington Post*, Nov. 9, 2018.

256 McCammond, "The Incumbents."

257 "Gubernatorial Elections 2018," Ballotpedia.

of Obama is a seminal example of the change that voters can bring about when hope leads to action.

Former President John F. Kennedy stands as another reminder that voters can change the country in powerful ways. While it may seem uneventful today, the election of President Kennedy was a significant event. Voters showed the impact they can have by electing the first Catholic President of the United States.

These examples demonstrate that you and I, We the People, can make a difference. They debunk the myth that all is lost and nothing can be changed. In today's political environment in which Washington and its elected officials have run amok, it is important to remind ourselves that we can make a difference…if we get involved.

We are the country that gained its independence by overcoming great odds breaking away from the world's superpower when most thought it couldn't be done. We swung the tide in World War II to stop the aggression of foreign adversaries trying to impose their will on us. In 1969, we broke the bonds of Earth's gravity, again overcoming great odds, this time to land a man on the moon. We are the country that overcomes and achieves greatness. With so much room for improvement, we have every reason to make that effort again, an effort that will be rewarded with America achieving its great economic potential.